ETERNAL WISDOM
FROM THE DESERT

ETERNAL WISDOM FROM THE DESERT

Writings from the Desert Fathers

EDITED AND MILDLY MODERNIZED BY
HENRY L. CARRIGAN, JR.

PARACLETE PRESS
BREWSTER, MASSACHUSETTS

Unless otherwise designated, Scripture quotations are taken from the New
Revised Standard Version of the Bible, © 1989 by the Division of Christian
Education of the National Council of the Churches of Christ in the U.S.A. All
rights reserved. Used by permission.

Scripture quotations designated (KJV) are taken from the King James Version.

Library of Congress Cataloging-in Publication Data
Eternal wisdom from the desert : writings from the desert fathers / edited and
mildly modernized by Henry L. Carrigan, Jr.
     p. cm.
    ISBN 1-55725-283-1
1. Desert Fathers. 2. Spiritual life—Christianity—History of doctrines—Early
church, ca. 30-600. I. Carrigan, Henry L., 1954–
BR 195.C5 E74 2001
270.1—dc21   2001003993

10 9 8 7 6 5

© 2001 by Paraclete Press
ISBN: 978-1-55725-283-8

Published by Paraclete Press
Brewster, Massachusetts
www.paracletepress.com
Printed in the United States of America.

Contents

Introduction

Two of the most enduring images used to describe the Christian spiritual life are the wilderness and the desert. On one level, Christians have used these images to describe spiritual experiences involving feelings of God's absence or abandonment. Christians often describe their feelings of spiritual loneliness and times of separation from God as periods of wandering in the wilderness. Often these same Christians, feeling that God is somehow testing them as they experience devastating losses, physical pain, or spiritual forlornness, compare their time of suffering to Jesus' experience of being tested in the desert.

While these images often suggest an aridity of spirit, however, they also evoke powerful visions of renewal and redemption. In Exodus 16, as the Israelites murmur their threats at Moses for leading them into such a situation, God provides food and water for them and guides them into a new land of promise. In Matthew 4:1–11 (Mark 1:12–13; Luke 4:1–13), Jesus finds himself alone in the wilderness with the great tempter, Satan. After forty days and forty nights of what appear to be exhausting struggles, Jesus emerges from his desert period prepared to face the challenges of his forthcoming ministry. The wilderness stories of the Israelites and of Jesus provide the foundational narratives of desert spirituality in the Christian traditions.

The history of the earliest Christian communities after Jesus' life and ministry is indeed the story of a wilderness experience. Very soon after Jesus' death, according to the account in Acts, several of his followers were killed for preaching his message of a coming new kingdom of God. One of the persecutors, Saul of Tarsus, suddenly experienced conversion to the nascent Christian tradition (while in the desert), changed his name to Paul, and soon became one of the tradition's most ardent supporters. During a period of roughly twenty years or less, Paul and his followers established numerous churches throughout the Mediterranean region. In his letters, Paul offered his advice to several churches about internal doctrinal matters—what does it mean to be ekklesia, or church?—as well as about external matters—how should the church or Christians deal with the Roman government?

During the first four centuries of the Common Era, Christianity experienced tremendous persecution at the hands of the Roman Empire. Paul and the writers of the Gospels had already warned their communities that the coming of the new kingdom would be fraught with perils for the faithful (1 Thessalonians 3:1–5, 5:1–11; Mark 13). But as the early Jesus movement migrated into urban areas and established churches, it came increasingly into conflict with the Roman Empire, which required total obedience to its laws of emperor worship. With their belief in the coming new kingdom in which their own God would reign supreme, many Christians refused to submit to the Empire's insistence that the true God was the Roman emperor. With such refusals began a series of persecutions of Christians under a string of emperors from Nero to Diocletian.

When the persecution was at its height in the first two centuries of the Common Era, church theologians such as Justin, Irenaeus, and Origen encouraged faithfulness to the developing doctrine of the church as well as to the Lordship of Jesus Christ. For Justin, persecution provided the opportunity to show true faithfulness to Christ by dying for him in the manner in which he had died for his followers. Thus, during these centuries of the developing Christian community, martyrdom became its central expression of faith. Early Christian martyrs enacted their own desires to be united with God through their passionate defenses of their faith and through their deaths. The passion of the martyrs for their faith attracted many new converts to Christianity, and suddenly the community found itself engaged in internal arguments about baptism and the nature of a true Christian.

Yet, these internal arguments did not halt the growth of Christianity. In fact, some have claimed recently that Christianity continued to grow in spite of martyrdom because of the frequent tendency of Christians to intermarry with non-Christians in the Empire. Whatever the reasons, Christian communities experienced slow but steady growth between the second and fourth centuries. By the time of Constantine, who issued an edict of toleration that ended the persecution of Christians, the Christian church had grown so large that it confronted new problems. Suddenly, the church found itself not having to engage in a process of self-definition.

When the emperor Constantine came to power in the early part of the fourth century, he ushered in a new attitude toward the Christian religion. Constantine himself probably experienced some kind of conversion to Christianity in 312, when he attributed his victory over his rival to the deity he referred to as the Unconquered Sun. While many Christians believed that their God had given Constantine the victory, he did not differentiate between his monotheism and that of the Christians. Thus, he adopted the Christian cross as his battle symbol, and he placed the "Chi-Rho" symbol of Christ on his coins beginning in 315.

Moreover, the emperor thought of himself as a ruler whose duty was to establish and promote a united church. As the first Christian Roman ruler, Constantine supported the growth of the church. In order to repay Christians for the years of persecutions by the Empire, he built new churches and had new copies of the Bible made. For the first time in its history, the church began to flourish as both a religious and a political institution.

In this time of relative peace, several new developments occurred in the church. First, the absence of persecution provided ample time for local bishops to begin debating the essentials of the Christian faith. Most notably, a number of debates about the person and nature of Christ took place. In earlier centuries, Christians did not have the leisure to argue about whether Jesus was fully divine or fully human or about how his two natures commingled, if they indeed did, with one another. In 325 a church council convened at Nicaea to attempt to settle this question, and offered some tentative answers that could be accepted by most churches in the East.

Such ecumenical councils led to a second development in early Christianity: the establishment of orthodoxy. In response to both internal and external pressures, these councils sought to develop belief-statements that would promote Christian self-definition. These creeds contained a number of doctrinal propositions to which believing Christians were required to assent as a proof of their right belief (orthodoxy). Those who could not assent to the creedal formulations were labeled "heretics," and were ousted from the church and sometimes killed because of their disagreement. Thus, the Christian community, which had fought so long against the persecution of the Empire, now began to persecute its own members for their unwillingness to agree with the doctrines the councils had established as the essentials that defined a Christian. For the outside world, the creeds functioned as documents of self-identification; for the church, the creeds defined orthodoxy.

Finally, as Christianity grew comfortable in its role as the official religion of the Roman Empire, many Christians became less and less comfortable with the church's too easy adopting of the culture. In the eyes of these believers, the church's new focus on establishing doctrinal correctness, along with its emphasis on creating a clerical hierarchy to monitor such orthodoxy, neglected the missionary impulse of the earliest Christian communities. Moreover, the passionate commitment of the martyrs to their faith was lost in the wrangling of the bishops and priests over fine philosophical points of theological doctrine. In addition, many Christians expressed deep dissatisfaction that the role of bishop, originally a religious office as set out in the New Testament, now involved obeisance to the Empire that had once persecuted Christians. Since the bishop now functioned as a political figure, many of his religious decisions favored the Empire rather than the church. This comfortable relationship with the emperor also meant that the church received financial support from the Empire, and the Christian church suddenly expanded into an institution whose too easy association with Rome corrupted it in the eyes of many of its congregants.

Many of these dissatisfied Christians began to flee the church in search of a purer form of Christianity untainted by collusion with empire. Thinking that they could return to an earlier expression of Christianity, these individuals fled the church in order to live lives of solitude and prayer as they sought to recapture the passion of second-century Christians for their faith. Thus, monasticism, perhaps the greatest movement to come out of the fourth–century church, developed and flourished.

But the Eastern, eremitic monasticism of the later fourth century is not the cenobitic (community) monasticism familiar to so many Western Christians. To be sure, these early monks practiced various forms of asceticism, and they saw themselves as returning to Christianity the kind of pure expression of faith that they thought was missing in the fourth-century church. Yet, these monks formed no communities with rules of faith and life that governed their practice. They did not congregate in monasteries and meet to observe fixed hours of prayer. Nor did they participate in the transmission of biblical texts through copying them, as later monks did. Rather, these monks were individuals who fled to the caves in the Egyptian desert to seek ecstatic union with God. One scholar observes that this "ascetical theology was a theology dominated by the ideal of the martyr who hoped for nothing in this world but sought for union with God in his passion."[1] These individuals usually renounced their material possessions and practiced a deep degree of self-sacrifice that recalled the spirit of Christians facing persecution in the earliest Christian communities. As with later monastic communities, the foundational elements of these monks' lives were chastity, abstinence, and unceasing prayer.

By the end of the fourth century, thousands of these hermits had settled along the length of the Nile River, and nearly 5,000 had established themselves in the desert on the outskirts of Alexandria. While they formed no distinct group or movement, these individuals later came to be known as the desert fathers, even though women also practiced this eremitic lifestyle. So powerful was the wisdom and purity of these desert monks that Christians from urban congregations continually streamed to the monks' caves seeking sagacious words of advice. Visitors to the monks' cells, or prayer chambers, addressed them with this formula: "Speak to me a word, Father, that I may live." The monks' answers were gathered early on in the collection called *Paradise* or *Apothegms of the Fathers* or, in most modern editions, *The Sayings*

---

1 Henry Chadwick. *The Early Church* (London: Penguin, 1967), 177.

of the Desert Fathers. Later generations of monks used these wise sayings and stories, which were sometimes directed to specific situations in a particular city, congregation, or monastic setting, as the basis for their own monastic life. For example, Basil of Caesarea and later Benedict of Nursia and John Cassian incorporated many of the teachings of the desert fathers into their monastic rules.

Several of the fathers became so famous for their wisdom and their acts that their contemporaries, or near-contemporaries, wrote biographies of these great hermits. Perhaps the most famous of the desert fathers was Antony of Egypt (251–356), who lived to be 105 years old. Not long after Antony's death, Athanasius, bishop of Alexandria, wrote an account of Antony's life that soon became a model for all other early Christian biographies. Athanasius' book appears to have become an immediate bestseller and to have remained one up through the Middle Ages. In his *Confessions*, Augustine remarks on the power of Athanasius' *Life of Antony*: "They found there a book in which was written the life of Antony. One of them began to read it. He was amazed and set on fire, and during his reading began to think of taking up this way of life and leaving his secular post in the civil service to be your servant." Indeed, Antony's conversion experience and his decision to become a monk bear remarkable similarities to Augustine's later description of his own conversion, though Athanasius' account is not nearly as theologically, or psychologically, freighted as is Augustine's.

When he was eighteen, Antony's parents died, leaving him all their property and wealth, as well as the responsibility of bringing up his younger sister. Not long after this event, he heard a preacher reading Matthew 19:21–22: "If you wish to be perfect, go, sell your possessions, and give the money to the poor, and you will have treasure in heaven." He went immediately and sold all his possessions, giving the money to the poor, but keeping just what he and his sister needed to live a frugal life.

Antony soon heard another preacher reading Matthew 6:34: "So do not worry about tomorrow, for tomorrow will bring worries of its own. Today's trouble is enough for today." Sorry that he had not obeyed God's direction fully from the beginning, Antony situated his sister in a convent, gave up the rest of his belongings, and dedicated his life to God's service. He then set out for the desert, where he ensconced himself in a series of caves and cells, moving farther and farther away from populated villages.

According to Athanasius' biography, Antony's days were filled with unceasing prayer and self-sacrifice. He found himself tormented by the harsh conditions of the desert, and he was often confronted with wild animals, which sometimes were demons in disguise. In a mirror of Jesus' temptations during his forty days in the wilderness, Satan and his minions tempted Antony often and arduously. Satan and his demons disguised themselves as beautiful creatures and as terrifying animals to test Antony's faithfulness to God. These tempters also placed enticing material possessions in Antony's path in hopes that the monk would succumb to the greedy desire to possess such goods. Eventually, Satan left Antony alone because the monk's relationship to God was so strong that he could not be moved.

Although Antony preferred to remain in solitude, his fame nevertheless spread far and wide, so that even Constantine wrote him a letter seeking counsel. Pilgrims flooded to see this great man of God and to solicit his wisdom. In addition to his teachings on chastity and the ascetic life, Antony reminded those who sought his advice to love one another, to avoid gossip and lies, and to avoid heresies such as the Arian belief that Jesus is not of the same substance as God.

There has been some question as to whether or not Antony was the first desert hermit. Antony himself mentioned that he sought out an old man for advice about an eremitic vocation. Whether or not this man was Paul the Hermit (d. 342), Antony claimed that he had "seen Paul in paradise." St. Jerome, most famous for his Latin translation of the Bible, the Vulgate, wrote a brief biography of Paul in the fifth century. Many contend that Jerome's purpose was to show that Paul had really been the first desert hermit.

Whatever Jerome's purpose, we do have one more brief biography of a famous desert father. Like Antony, Paul left for the desert at a young age—in Paul's case, sixteen. The highlight of Jerome's *Life of Paul* is the encounter between Antony and Paul, where the two embrace warmly and discuss briefly the eremitic life. In a story reminiscent of the Old Testament tale of Elijah and Elisha, at his death Paul passes his cloak to Antony much as Elijah passes along his mantle of prophecy to Elisha.

The Sayings of the Desert Fathers contain the collected wisdom of these desert hermits. While none of them gained the fame or notoriety of Paul or Antony, each monk had his own followers who sought sagacious advice from him. Unfortunately, little is known about many of these figures, for no biographical material is recorded for most of them. One of the better known was John the Dwarf, who was born about 339. When John was eighteen, he traveled to Scetis to be trained by Father Ammoes. In order to preserve his solitude, he dug himself an underground cave. Yet another well-known hermit was Evagrius, who spent ten years as a disciple of Macarius of Alexandria and was famous for his scholarship and rigorous asceticism. He produced two works on the ascetic life, *Praktikos* and *Chapters on Prayer*. Whether famous or not, each of the desert fathers passionately sought union with

God and taught those who came to them the values of constant prayer, fasting, Scripture reading, and love.

What do the desert fathers have to say to us today? It's clear that most contemporary Christians cannot practice the severe asceticism of the desert fathers, nor do they desire to do so. Many cannot leave home and family to strike off into remote wilderness areas in order to seek ecstatic union with God. In fact, as monasticism developed, so did the divide between the professional contemplatives—that is, those called to the monastic vocation as a way of life—and those Christians who remained a part of society and lived their vocations in the midst of the messiness of everyday life. While the former sometimes condemned the latter, and the latter often admired the former, the commitment to ascetic practices was transformed into daily rituals that could be woven into the fabric of daily life.

Thus, the desert fathers act as guides to the interior life. In their sayings and in their lives, they counsel humility, prayer, patience, and introspection. The desert fathers teach us that deep contemplative practice provides eternal wisdom for our daily lives.

A Word About the Text

Athanasius' *Life of Antony* can be found in *The Nicene and Post-Nicene Fathers*, Second Series, Vol. 6 (Grand Rapids: Eerdmans). For Jerome's *Life of Paul of Thebes*, I have also used the translation available in *The Nicene and Post-Nicene Fathers*, Vol. 4. The Penguin edition of *Early Christian Lives* (1998), edited by Carolinne White, has proved enormously useful in providing background materials of these biographies. Henry Chadwick's *The Early Church* (London: Penguin, 1967) remains a superb introduction to the period in which the desert fathers lived and worked. I have also used Helen Waddell's *The Desert Fathers* (London: Constable & Co., 1936), supplemented by Benedicta Ward's *The Sayings of the Desert Fathers* (Kalamazoo, Michigan: Cistercian, 1975). The selection of the sayings of the desert fathers in this Paraclete edition comprises a very small portion of the huge number of sayings available. However, I have not included most of the longer apothegms, and I have left out stories and sayings that are specific to particular issues concerning the monastic life.

I have remained true to the spirit of the text even where I have mildly modernized it. I have replaced archaic words where necessary. Thus, for the word "cell," which is simply a monk's dwelling place but which today has other connotations, I have used "prayer chamber." I have altered the syntax and sentence structure of the sayings and the biographies to make them livelier and more appealing to a contemporary audience. Most often this simply means casting sentences in the active rather than the passive voice.

I trust that the words of the desert fathers will speak to you today even as they spoke to Christians thousands of years ago.

Henry L. Carrigan, Jr.
Lancaster, Pennsylvania
Lent 2001

The Life of Antony of Egypt

by Athanasius

✠

PREFACE

Athanasius addresses his life of Antony to monks in Europe:

You have entered into an admirable contest by seeking to equal or outdo the monks of Egypt in striving for moral perfection through strict self-discipline. May God fulfill this desire for you.

You asked me to write about Antony's life. You want to know about his early life, and what his life was like before he dedicated himself to God. You want to know also about the end of Antony's life and whether or not the legends you've heard about him are true, so that you may imitate him. I write this biography joyously, since Antony shows us the perfect path to virtue. The memory of Antony's life and work enriches me and encourages you to follow his example.

You should believe everything you hear about Antony. He performed extraordinary works, and you have until now only heard about the least remarkable ones. For even I do not know everything about him, and I will not be able to tell you accurately everything about his exceptional character. If you want to know more of Antony's merits, you must ask questions of those you meet from Egypt, for they will tell you all they know about him and provide a full account of Antony's remarkable life. But since you may not have the chance to talk with these people, I have written down for you those things I know myself—for I visited him often—and those I learned from a person who spent a good deal of time with him. I hope that from my account you will learn the truth about Antony. If I tell you too many things, you might be skeptical of his miracles. I also do not want to you to hear any words that are not justified by Antony's merits, for I don't want you to think of this man as incapable of performing a miracle despite his great reputation.

✠

LIFE OF ANTONY

1.   Antony, then, came from Egypt; he was the son of well-born and devout parents. He was brought up so carefully by his family that he knew nothing apart from his parents and his home. While he was still a boy, he refused to learn to read and write or to join in the silly games of the other little children. Instead, he burned with a desire for God and lived a life of simplicity at home, as the Bible says of Jacob. He also often went with his parents to church but did not fool around as little children tend to, nor did he show a lack of respect as young boys often do. He concentrated on what was being read and put the useful precepts into practice in his way of life. He was never a nuisance to his family, as children usually are because of their desire for a variety of dainty foods. He did not long for the pleasures of more delicate food; he was content with just what he was given and asked for nothing more.

2.   When he and his little sister were left completely on their own after their parents died (Antony was around eighteen

years old), he took good care of his house and his sister. Before six months had passed, though, he was on his way to church one day when he thought about how the apostles had rejected everything to follow the Savior. He thought about how the early Christians had sold their possessions and laid the proceeds at the apostles' feet to distribute to the needy. What great hope was stored up for those people in heaven! As he was thinking about these things, Antony entered the church. As he went into the church, he heard this Gospel being read: *If you wish to be perfect, go, sell your possessions and give the money to the poor, and you will have treasure in heaven; then come, follow me* (Matthew 19:21).

When he heard this, Antony applied the Lord's commandment to himself, believing that because of divine inspiration he had first remembered the incident and that this Scripture was being read aloud for his sake. He immediately went home and sold the possessions he owned. He possessed 300 fertile acres that he shared among his neighbors to prevent anyone from bearing a grudge against him or his sister. All the rest of his possessions, which were movable goods, he sold. The great profit he made from the sale of these goods he gave to the poor. He kept a little for his sister's sake, because she seemed more vulnerable on account of her youth.

3.   On another occasion when Antony had gone to church and heard the Lord saying in the Gospel: *Do not worry about tomorrow, for tomorrow will bring worries of its own* (Matthew 6:34), he shared all the rest of his wealth with the poor. He was not content to stay at home, but he left his sister to be brought up by some faithful and good women. Now free from all worldly ties, he entered into a harsh and severe life. There were not yet many monasteries in Egypt at the time, and

there was no one who was familiar with the remote desert. People who wanted to serve Christ settled at a distance from their own villages. On a neighboring estate there was an old man who had lived a solitary life since his youth. When Antony saw this old man, Antony wanted more than anything to imitate the man's goodness. When he started out, Antony lived in places that were not too far from his home. Later, though, whenever he heard about someone who was engaged in this disciplined life, Antony would go out and search for him. He would not return home until he had seen the person he longed to see. After he began in this way, his resolve grew stronger every day until he reached the point where he no longer thought of his family wealth or of his relatives. He focused his desire and his attention on the task he had undertaken, and worked with his hands. For he knew that the Bible teaches that anyone unwilling to work should not eat. Apart from what he needed for bread, the money he earned he gave to the poor. He prayed often, for he had learned that he should pray to the Lord constantly. He also listened intently to the Scriptures so that none of its lessons would be lost on him. He preserved all the Lord's commandments in his memory.

4. He led his life in such a way that all the brothers loved him with a pure love. He obeyed everyone whom he visited. Eager to learn, he assimilated their various individual gifts. He imitated the self-restraint of one, the cheerfulness of another. He emulated the gentleness of one, the nocturnal devotions of another, and the dedication in reading of yet another. He admired one who fasted and another who slept on the bare ground, praising the endurance of the former and the compassion of the latter. He kept in mind the love they all showed one another, and he returned to his own place

refreshed by every aspect of their virtues. There he would ponder all he had learned and try to imitate the good points of each one. He was never provoked to anger. The only fire that burned in his heart was his determination to excel in the deeds just mentioned. He did this in such a way that he was dear to them all, even though he surpassed them in glory. When his neighbors and those monks whom he visited often saw him, they called him God's friend. Some loved him as a son; others loved him as a brother.

5. While Antony was busy with doing all these things that caused so many to love him, the devil, who could not bear to see a young man with such outstanding virtues, began to attack him. First, he tried to drag Antony away from the life to which he had committed himself. He made Antony remember his wealth, his sister's protection, and his family's social status. The devil tried to stimulate in Antony a desire for material things, the short-lived honors of this world, the pleasures of different kinds of food, and many other attractions that belong to an indulgent life. He reminded Antony of the great difficulty in obtaining the life of virtue. He also reminded him of the body's weakness. He created great confusion in Antony's thoughts, hoping to call him back from his intentions. But when, as result of Antony's prayers to God, the devil realized that he had been driven out by Antony's faith in Christ's sufferings, he seized the weapons with which he normally attacks all young people, using seductive dreams to disturb Antony. First he tried to unsettle him at night by means of hostile hordes and terrifying sounds, and then he attacked him by day with weapons that were so obviously his that no one could doubt that Antony was fighting against the devil. For the devil tried to implant dirty thoughts, but Antony pushed them away by means of constant prayer. The

devil tried to titillate his senses by means of natural carnal desires, but Antony defended his whole body by faith, by praying at night, and by fasting. At night the devil would turn himself into the attractive form of a beautiful woman, omitting no detail that might provoke lascivious thoughts, but Antony called to mind the fiery punishment of hell. In this way he resisted the onslaught of lust. The devil without hesitation set before him the slippery path of youth that leads to disaster, but Antony concentrated on the everlasting torments of future judgment and kept his soul's purity untainted throughout these temptations. All these things confounded the devil. A young man was now tricking this evil creature who thought he could become God's equal, as if the devil himself were a wretched creature. A man made of flesh defeated the devil, who tries to defeat flesh and blood. The Lord, who became flesh for our sake and thus granted the body victory over the devil, was helping Antony.

6. At last the devil found he was unable to destroy Antony and that Antony's thoughts were always driving him back. So, crying and gnashing his teeth, he appeared to Antony in a form appropriate to his nature. An ugly dark boy threw himself down at Antony's feet, weeping loudly and saying in a human voice, "I have led many astray, and I have deceived many, but you have defeated my efforts, just as other holy people have done." When Antony asked him who was saying this, the devil replied, "I am the friend of sin. I have used many different kinds of shameful weapons to attack young people, and that is why I am called the spirit of sinfulness. How many of those who were determined to live chastely have I tricked! How many times have I persuaded those starting out hesitantly to return to their former foul ways. I am the one who caused the prophet to reproach the fallen, saying,

The spirit of sinfulness has led you astray (cf. Hosea 4:12), and I am the one who made them fall. I am the one who has often tempted you, and always you have driven me away." When the soldier of Christ heard this, he gave thanks to God and, strengthened by greater confidence in the face of the enemy, he said, "You are utterly despicable and contemptible; your blackness and your age are signs of weakness. You do not worry me any longer. *The Lord is on my side to help me; I shall look in triumph on those who hate me*" (Psalm 118:7). At the sound of Antony's singing, the apparition immediately vanished.

7. This was Antony's first victory over the devil. It was the first sign of the Savior's power in Antony. The Savior *condemned sin in the flesh, so that the just requirement of the law might be fulfilled in us, who walk not according to the flesh but according to the Spirit* (Romans 8:4). But this triumph did give Antony a sense of security. The devil's powers did not fail completely. The devil, like a roaring lion, was always watching for some way to pounce on Antony. Knowing from the Bible that the devil's wiles are numerous, Antony kept his commitment firm by skillful effort. Antony realized that although Satan had been defeated in the struggles of the flesh, he could use new strategies and more deadly weapons against him. Thus Antony disciplined his body more and more, afraid that he, who had won some contests, might lose others. He thus began to live a more rigorous rule of life. Even though everyone was amazed at this young man's tireless dedication, Antony endured his discipline patiently because he knew that voluntary servitude to God would transform habit into nature.

8. Antony so endured hunger and sleeplessness that his powers were considered astonishing. He very often spent the entire night in prayer and ate only once a day, after sunset. Sometimes he continued fasting for two or three days at a

time and only ate and drank on the fourth day. He ate bread and salt, and drank a little water. I think it is better not to say anything about his consumption of meat and wine, for most monks do not consume either one. When he did allow himself to rest, he used a woven rush mat covered with goats' hair. Sometimes he would simply lie on the bare ground, and he refused to anoint his body with oil. For he used to say that it is hardly possible that the bodies of those who use such things, and especially young men's bodies, should grow strong if they are softened by smooth oil. Instead they ought to use rigorous exercises to control the flesh, as the Apostle Paul said: *Therefore I am content with weaknesses, insults, hardships, persecutions, and calamities for the sake of Christ; for whenever I am weak, then I am strong* (2 Corinthians 12:10). Antony also stated that wearing down the body's energies in this way could revive a person's mental powers. That is the reason he did not measure the value of his tasks by the length of time spent, but with the love and willing servitude characteristic of a novice. He continued to maintain his desire to progress in the fear of God. Wanting to add new achievements to the old ones, he kept in mind Paul's words: *Forgetting what lies behind and straining forward to what lies ahead, I press on toward the goal for the prize of the heavenly call of God in Christ Jesus* (Philippians 3:13). He remembered also what Elijah said: *As the Lord of hosts lives, before whom I stand, I will surely show myself to him today* (1 Kings 18:15). Antony explained that "today" did not mean just past time but that every day he was entering battle, and he wanted to prove himself worthy in God's sight, pure of heart, and ready to obey God's will.

9. Then the holy Antony, bearing in mind that a servant of God should organize his life based on the life of the great Elijah, moved away to some tombs not far from his own village. He

asked one of his friends to bring him food at regular intervals. When this brother had shut him up in one of the tombs, Antony remained there alone. But the devil was afraid that the desert might become inhabited because of Antony, so he gathered his followers and tortured Antony by beating him all over. The intensity of the pain deprived Antony of his ability to move and speak. At a later time he would tell how his injuries had been so serious that they were worse than all the tortures devised by other men. However, God's providence saved him. The next day the brother arrived with food as usual and found the tomb's door smashed down and Antony lying half-dead on the ground. He lifted him on his shoulders and carried him back to his house in the village. When people heard about this, many neighbors and relatives came running and in their grief performed the funeral rites for Antony. When the night was half over, a deep weariness overcame those keeping watch. Then Antony, his spirit gradually returning, drew a deep breath and lifted his head. When he saw that the man who had brought him there was awake while all the others were lying fast asleep, he beckoned to the man and begged him to carry him back, without waking anyone at all, to the place where he had been living.

10. So Antony was carried back to his tomb, and stayed there alone as he had before. Since he could not stand up because of his recent beatings, he prayed lying down. After praying, Antony would say in a loud voice, "Look, here I am. I don't run away from fighting with you. Even if you bring me more difficulties, you cannot separate me from Christ's love." And he would then chant these words: *Though an army encamp against me, my heart shall not fear* (Psalm 27:3). When he heard this, the devil was amazed that Antony had dared to come back. The devil was furious. Gathering his dogs together, he

said to them, "See how Antony is overcome neither by the spirit of sinfulness nor by physical pain. To top it all off, he is disrespectful in his challenges to us. Take up all your weapons; we must attack with greater force. Let him feel, let him feel; he must understand who it is that he is provoking." When the devil spoke, all those listening to him agreed with him, for the devil has immeasurable ways of doing harm. Then there was a sudden noise that caused the place to shake violently. Holes appeared in the wall, and a swarm of different kinds of demons poured out. They took on the shape of wild animals and snakes, and instantly they filled the whole place with apparitions in the form of lions, bulls, wolves, vipers, serpents, scorpions, leopards, and bears. They each made noises according to their individual natures: The lion roared, eager for the kill; the bull bellowed and made menacing movements with his horns; the serpent hissed; the wolves leaped forward to attack; the spotted leopard showed all the different wiles of the one that controlled him. Each of their faces bore a savage expression, and the sound of their voices was terrifying. Mauled and beaten, Antony experienced even more atrocious pains in his body; but he remained unafraid, and his mind was alert. Although the wounds of his flesh made him groan, he maintained the same attitude and spoke as if mocking his enemies: "If you had any power, one of you would be enough for the fight; but since the Lord has robbed you of your strength, you are broken and so you attempt to use large numbers to terrify me. The proof of your weakness is that you have taken on the shapes of unreasoning beasts." He continued to speak with confidence: "If you truly have any influence, if the Lord has granted you any power over me, here I am: Eat me up. But if you cannot, why do you use up so much energy? For the sign of the cross and faith in the

Lord is for us a wall that no assault of yours can break down."
Although they made numerous threats against the holy
Antony, they did not succeed. They made fools of them-
selves, not of Antony.

11. Jesus did not fail to notice his servant's struggle. He came to
protect Antony. When Antony raised his eyes, he saw the
roof opening above him. As the darkness dissipated, a ray of
light poured in on him. As soon as this bright light appeared,
all the demons vanished, and the pain in Antony's body suddenly stopped. The building that had been destroyed was
restored. Antony immediately understood that the Lord was
present. Sighing deeply from the bottom of his heart, he
spoke to the light that had appeared to him: "Where were
you, good Jesus? Where were you? Why weren't you here
from the beginning to heal my wounds?" And a voice came to
him: "Antony, I was here, but I was waiting to watch your
struggle. But now, since you have bravely held your own in
this fight, I will always help you and I will make you famous
throughout the world." When he heard this, Antony stood up
and prayed; he felt so greatly strengthened that he realized
he had received more strength now than he had before he
lost it. Antony was thirty-five years old when this happened.

12. Later, as his willing commitment caused him to grow in spiritual goodness, he went to the old man I mentioned earlier
and begged that they should live together in the desert.
When the old man refused, giving as his excuse his old age
and the novelty of the plan, Antony went forth to the mountain
alone, having lost all fear of that way of life, and attempted
to open up a path to the desert that had before now been
unknown to the monks. However, not even there did his
tireless adversary give up. Determined to obstruct Antony's
commitment to this way of life, the devil threw down a silver

plate in his path. When Antony saw it, he recognized the cunning of that ingenious trickster. He stood still and fearless, and, looking at the plate grimly, he rebuked the one trying to trick him with the illusion of silver. He said to himself, "Why is this plate here in the desert? This track is remote and there are no traces of any travelers. If it had fallen out of someone's luggage, it could hardly have lain unnoticed, for it is too large. If the person who lost it came back, he would certainly have found what had fallen out because this place is so empty. This is a product of your cunning, you devil, but you will not hinder my intention. May your silver plate go to hell with you." As soon as Antony said this, the plate disappeared like smoke from the face of the fire.

13. Next Antony saw a piece of real gold lying in his path. It is not clear whether the devil put it there to deceive him, or whether God revealed it to prove that Antony could not be seduced even by real riches. Antony marveled at the size of this piece of shining metal and quickly ran all the way to the mountain, as if he were escaping from a fire. After crossing the river, he found a deserted fort full of venomous animals. He settled in the fort as its new tenant. Immediately on his arrival, a huge number of snakes fled as if they had been chased out. Antony then blocked up the entrance with stones and stayed there all alone, storing up enough bread for six months as well as a small supply of water. He did not go out to receive any visitors. Even when he took his bread supply through the roof twice a year, he did not talk with those who brought it to him.

14. When crowds of people spent the night outside his door so they could question him, they heard noisy voices as if a number of people were saying to Antony, "Why have you moved into our home? What have you got to do with the desert?

Leave other people's property alone. You cannot live here;
you cannot endure our attacks." At first those outside thought
some people had entered the walls and were quarreling with
Antony. But when they looked in through the gaps, they saw
no one and realized demons were fighting Antony. They
were terribly frightened and called to Antony for help. He
came to the door to comfort the brothers; he begged them
not to be afraid and asked them to go away. He assured them
that their fear was caused by the demons. "Make the sign of
the cross," he said, "and leave without fear. Leave these
demons to mock themselves." So the people returned to their
homes while Antony remained there unharmed, never tiring
in his struggle. For he increased in his commitment, and the
weakness of his opponents accorded him the greatest relief in
his fight and made him steadfast of mind. When crowds of
people came to the desert again, they expected to find him
dead. But he sang from within, *Let God rise up, let his enemies be
scattered; let those who hate him flee before him. As smoke is driven away,
so drive them away; as wax melts before the fire, let the wicked perish before
God* (Psalm 68:1–2). He also sang, *All nations surrounded me; in the
name of the Lord I cut them off!* (Psalm 118:10).

15. Antony spent twenty years in the desert in this way, staying
out of humankind's sight. Many came to see him in their
desire to imitate his commitment to his way of life. A number
of people who were suffering also gathered outside his door.
When they at last managed to tear down the doors by force,
Antony appeared to them with an aura of holiness as if he had
emerged from some divine sanctuary. Everyone was stunned
at the beauty of his expression and the dignified bearing of
his body, which had not grown weak through lack of exercise. His face had not grown pale as the result of fasting and
fighting with demons. To the contrary, his body looked as if

no time had passed. What a great miracle. What purity of mind he had. Never did excessive frivolity cause him to burst out laughing; never did the thought of past sins make him frown, nor did the high praise bestowed on him by his admirers make him conceited. The solitude had in no way made him uncivilized, and the daily battles with his enemies had not brutalized him. His mind was calm, and he maintained a well-balanced attitude in all situations. Then the grace of God, through Antony, freed many people from unclean spirits and from various illnesses. His speech brought comfort to those who were grieving, instructed the ignorant, reconciled those who were angry, and persuaded everyone that nothing should be valued higher than Christ's love. He set before their eyes the great number of future rewards as well as the mercy of God, and he made known the benefits granted because God did not spare His own Son but had given him for the salvation of us all. His words had the immediate effect of persuading many of those who heard him to reject human things. This was the beginning of the colonization of the desert.

16. I should also mention what happened in the region of Arsinoe. Antony planned to visit the brothers there. He had to swim across the Nile River, which was full of crocodiles and other dangerous animals. He and his companions crossed the river without harm and returned safely, too. After that he continued steadfastly in his ascetic efforts, and he inspired many of the brothers by his teaching. In a short time a large number of monastic prayer chambers came into existence. He guided these monks with a fatherly affection.

17. One day, when the brothers who had gathered there were asking the holy Antony to provide some guidelines for their way of life, he raised his voice with a prophet's confidence

and said that the Scriptures were sufficient for all teaching of the rule. He taught also that it would be an excellent idea for the brothers to support each other with mutual encouragement. "And so," he said, "you should tell me, as if I were your father, what you have learned, and I will reveal to you, as if you were my sons, what I have discovered as a result of my great age. But let this be the first rule, shared by all of you, that no one should weaken in the firmness of his commitment to the way of life he has chosen. He should strive always to increase his commitment to this undertaking as if he were just starting out, especially because human life, compared to eternity, is very short." After beginning in this way, Antony was silent for a while. Marveling at God's great generosity, he then added, "In this present life, things of equal value are exchanged: The seller does not receive more from the buyer. But the promise of eternal life is brought at a low price. As it is written: *The days of our life are seventy years, or perhaps eighty if we are strong; even then their span is only toil and trouble; they are soon gone, and we fly away* (Psalm 90:10). If we have lived in God's work for eighty or a hundred years, working hard, we will not reign for the same amount of time in the future. Instead, in exchange for the years I mentioned, we shall be granted a reign lasting throughout all ages. It is not earth that we will inherit, but heaven. We shall leave this corrupt body and we shall receive it incorrupt.

18. "And so, my children, do not let yourselves grow weary. Do not be seduced by pride in your achievement. *For the sufferings of this present time are not worth comparing with the glory about to be revealed to us* (Romans 8:18). No one, once he has rejected this world, should think he has left behind anything important. The entire earth, compared to the infinity of the heavens, is small and limited. Even if we renounce the whole world, we

cannot give anything in exchange that is of similar value to the heavenly dwellings. If each person considers this, he will immediately realize that if he abandons a few acres of land or a small house or a moderate sum of gold, he ought not to feel proud of himself in the belief that he has given up a lot. Nor should he become despondent, thinking that he will receive only a little in return. For just as someone considers one dollar of no value in comparison with winning one hundred dollars, so, too, anyone who renounces possession of the entire world will receive in heaven a hundred times as much in more valuable rewards. In short, we must realize that even if we want to retain our riches, we will be torn away from them against our will by the law of death, as it says in Ecclesiastes. Why then do we not make a virtue of necessity? Why do we not voluntarily abandon what must be destroyed when this light comes to an end, so that we might gain the kingdom of heaven? Let Christians care for nothing that they cannot take away with them. We ought rather to seek after that which will lead us to heaven, namely wisdom, chastity, justice, virtue, an ever-watchful mind, care of the poor, firm faith in Christ, a mind that can control anger, and hospitality. Striving after these things, we shall prepare for ourselves a dwelling in the land of the peaceful, as it says in the Gospel.

19. "Let us bear in mind that we are servants of the Lord and that we owe a service to him who created us. For a servant does not reject present or future authority on account of past service, and does not dare to claim that because of his past he ought to be released from the task at hand. Instead, he continues to perform the same service with unbroken commitment so as to please his master and so that his wages will not be fear and beatings. In the same way it is right for us to obey the divine commandments, knowing that he who is a just

judge will judge each person where he finds him, as the prophet Ezekiel testifies. Even the wretched Judas, because of one night's sins, lost out on the rewards for all his past achievement.

20. "We must therefore be steadily committed to this way of life with God as our helper, for it is written: *We know that all things work together for good for those who love God* (Romans 8:28). Let us reflect on the Apostle's claim that he dies each day, so that we can avoid idleness. If we bear in mind the unpredictability of our human condition, we will not sin. For when we wake from sleep, we are unsure whether we will reach evening, and when we lie down to rest at night, we should not be confident that daylight will return. We should be aware always of the uncertainty of our life and know that we are governed by God's providence. Not only will we not go astray nor be swept away by some flimsy desire, but neither will we be angry with anyone nor strive to accumulate earthly treasures. Instead, fearing death each day and always thinking about our separation from the body, we will trample upon all that is transitory. The desire for women will disappear, the fire of lust will be extinguished, and we will pay our debts to each other, always holding before our eyes the coming of the final retribution. For a powerful fear of judgment and a terrible dread of punishment destroy the incentives of the lustful flesh and support the soul as it slips off the cliff's edge.

21. "I pray then that we should use every effort to press on toward this life's goal. Let no one look behind him as did Lot's wife, especially since the Lord has said that no one who puts his hand upon the plough and looks back is fit for the kingdom of heaven. To look back means to have second thoughts about your undertaking and to become entangled once more in worldly desires. Do not fear the word 'virtue' as if it were

unattainable. Do not think that such an endeavor, which depends on our will, is alien to you or something remote. Man has a natural inclination to this kind of effort, and it is something that awaits only our willingness. Let the Greeks pursue their studies across the seas and go in search of teachers of useless literature in foreign lands. We, however, feel no compulsion to travel across the waves, for the kingdom of heaven is to be found everywhere on earth. That is why the Lord says in the Gospel: *The kingdom of God is among you* (Luke 17:21). The virtue that is within us requires only the human will. For who can doubt that the natural purity of the soul, were it not tainted by filth, would be the source of all virtues? A good Creator must necessarily have made the soul good. If we hesitate, we should hear the words of Joshua, who said, *Incline your hearts to the LORD, the God of Israel* (Joshua 24:33). And John expresses a similar idea about virtue when he says, *Make his paths straight* (Matthew 3:3). For to have a straight soul means that the blemish of any vices does not stain its original soundness. If it changes its nature, then it is said to have gone astray, but if it preserves its good nature, then that is virtue. The Lord has entrusted our soul to us: Let us keep what has been entrusted to us in the same state as it was in when we received it. No one can put forward as an excuse that what is born in him is external to him. Let him who made us recognize his own creation, and let him find his own work as he created it. Our natural adornment is enough for us: You who are human must not disfigure what divine generosity has granted you. To wish to alter the works of God is to desecrate them.

22. "We ought to be careful to ensure that we control the tyrannical passion of anger, since it says in the Bible, *Your anger does not produce God's righteousness* (James 1:20), and *Desire gives birth to*

sin, and that sin, when fully grown, gives birth to death (James 1:15). The divine voice has recommended that we should protect our soul with unceasing vigilance and lead it toward perfection with all care and effort, because we have enemies who are trained to trip us up. These are the demons whom we must fight without a truce, according to the testimony of the Apostle who says: *For our struggle is not against enemies of flesh and blood, but against the rulers, against the authorities, against the cosmic powers of this present darkness, against the spiritual forces of evil in the heavenly places* (Ephesians 6:12). Huge numbers of them are flying through the air here; the enemy troops are rushing all around us. I am not able to describe their diversity, so I shall leave this task to those who are more competent than I. I shall give a brief account, though, of the things one should be aware of, specifically the tricks the demons have devised against us.

23. "First of all, we should hold firm in our minds the fact that God has made nothing that is evil and that the demons did not derive their origin from any arrangement on his part. Their perversity is a fault not of nature but of the will. In fact they were good, in that God created them, but they fell to earth from heaven by their own will. Wallowing there in the filthy mire, they introduced the wicked worship of paganism. Now they are tortured by envy of us and never cease to devise every possible evil scheme to prevent us taking over the top positions they once held. But their wickedness is of various kinds, and they divide it among them. Some of them have reached the topmost summit of destructiveness, while others seem less harmful in comparison with the ones that are more wicked. They have all undertaken different struggles against different causes according to the strength of their demonic powers. That is why it is necessary to ask the Lord

to grant the ability to distinguish between spirits, so that we may see through their tricks and their efforts and raise the single banner of the Lord's cross in confronting the unequal battle. Paul showed that he had been granted this ability when he said, *And we do this so that we may not be outwitted by Satan, for we are not ignorant of his designs* (2 Corinthians 2:11). Following his example we, too, should use our own experiences to instruct each other in conversation.

24. "The demons are hostile to all Christians, but they especially hate those who are monks and nuns of Christ. They set traps along their paths and strive to undermine their commitment by means of irreverent and obscene thoughts, but do not let them strike terror into you. For the prayers and fasting of those who have faith in the Lord cause the demons to collapse immediately. But even if they are driven back a little way, do not think that you have gained complete victory. For they have a tendency, when wounded, to rise up with even greater violence and to change their method of attack. When they do not succeed with dirty thoughts, they use fears to terrify, transforming themselves into women one moment, wild animals the next moment, and then serpents, and finally turning into troops of soldiers and an infinite number of shapes. All these vanish as soon as the sign of the cross is made. When these means of deception have also been recognized, the demons begin to prophesy and to try to predict future events. But when they have been thwarted in these efforts, they summon the leader of their wickedness, the culmination of all evil, to assist them in their fight."

25. Antony often claimed that he had seen the devil looking as he did when the Lord revealed him to Job: *His eyes look like Venus and lamps of incense spark from his mouth. His hair is sprinkled with flames and smoke comes out of his nostrils, like a coal from the heat*

of a burning oven. His breath is like a glowing coal and a flame leaps forth from his mouth (cf. Job 41:18–21). "The prince of demons appeared in terrifying visions like this," Antony explained, "boasting and raging with his godless tongue. But the Lord triumphed over him, saying to Job: *He counts iron as straw and bronze as rotten wood* (Job 41:27). Through the prophet the devil boasts, saying: *I will pursue and overtake* (Exodus 15:9) and *I will hold the whole world in my hand like a nest and I shall take them away like eggs that have been abandoned* (cf. Isaiah 10:14). In this way the wicked one, by pouring forth deadly words, frequently ensnares some of those who live a good life. But we must not believe his promises or fear his threats, for he always deceives, and none of his promises are true. For if everything he says were not a lie, how is it that when he made such infinitely extravagant promises the Lord hooked him like a serpent, using the hook of the cross? How is it that he was bound with a halter like a beast of burden, and tied up in chains like a runaway slave, his lips pierced by an iron ring? How is it that he was not given the chance to devour any of the faithful at all? Now he is as miserable as a sparrow caught by Christ in the net to be mocked at; now he groans for his companions who have been trampled beneath the Christians' heels like scorpions and serpents. He who took pride in the fact that he would hold the world in his hand, look at him! You have conquered him, and notice how he is unable to prevent me from arguing with him. My dear ones, proud boastfulness must be completely rejected together with empty words. That brightness that pretends to shine is not the brightness of genuine light but is a sign of the flames with which he is to burn, for it disappears more swiftly than it can be told, taking with it the image of its own punishment.

26. "Often the demons sing the psalms while remaining invisible,

shocking as it is to tell. In addition they recite the sacred words of Scripture with a foul mouth, for often when we are reading, they repeat the last words like an echo. They also awaken to prayer those who are asleep, so as to deprive them of sleep for the whole night. They disguise themselves as genuine monks and put pressure on many of the monks, accusing them of their sins, in which the demons themselves were their accomplices. But you must reject their accusations as well as their advice to fast and their suggestions that you should stay awake, for they are deceiving you. They assume shapes familiar to us so that they may harm us through their resemblance to virtue. They think they can more easily inject their poison and destroy innocent people by means of seemingly admirable behavior. Finally, they claim that the monk's task is impossibly hard, hoping that the monks might come to regard what they have undertaken as too onerous, and that despair might then lead them to loss of enthusiasm, and loss of enthusiasm to failure of effort.

27. "And so the Lord sent the prophet to denounce these wretched creatures. He said, in a powerful voice, *Alas for you who make your neighbors drink, pouring out your wrath until they are drunk* (Habakkuk 2:15). By making suggestions like this, the demons seduce people from the path that leads them to heaven. When the Lord came to earth, the demons spoke the truth about him against their will. They said, *You are the Son of God* (Luke 4:41). He who freed the men who were tongue-tied shut their noisy mouths to prevent the demons' mixing in the poison of error with their announcement of the truth. The Lord also wanted us to follow Christ's example and to refuse to assent to the demons in any way, even if they persuade us of something that might be beneficial. For it is certainly not right for us, now that the Lord has granted freedom and the life-giving statements

The Life of Antony of Egypt   23

contained in the Scriptures, to accept advice on how to live from the devil, who deserted his own post and feared Christ's holy authority. And so the Lord ordered the devil to be quiet even when he was quoting from Scripture, because God says to the sinner, *What right have you to recite my statutes and take up my covenant on your lips?* (Psalm 50:16). The demons make all kinds of pretense: Often they chat with the brothers, often a host of them produce strange noises. They grab the monks' hands; they hiss and cackle inanely, so that they might enter the Christian's heart at the moment of sin. But when they are driven back by everyone, their wailing at last proves their weakness.

28. "But the Lord, because he is God and aware of his own authority, ordered them to be silent. We, however, should follow in the saints' footsteps and walk the same path as those who saw more clearly the tricks I have mentioned. They used to sing: *I will guard my ways that I may not sin with my tongue. . . . I was silent and still; I held my peace to no avail* (Psalm 39:1–2a) and *But I am like the deaf, I do not hear; like the mute, who cannot speak. Truly, I am like one who does not hear* (Psalm 38:13–14). Christ commanded silence because he is the Lord; we must overcome the devil by not believing in him. If they force us to pray, if they persuade us to fast, we should do this, not at their suggestion, but because it is part of our way of life. Even if they attack us and threaten us with death, we ought to laugh at them rather than fear them. For they are weak and cannot carry out all their threats.

29. "I am aware that I have already spoken in passing about these matters, but now I must explain all this in a fuller way, because repetition brings greater security. When the Lord came, the enemy was destroyed and all his power undermined. For this reason, when the devil sees that he has collapsed and

remembers his former strength, like a tyrant who is now growing old, he attacks human wickedness. However, even when he uses thoughts and other tricks he still cannot overcome a heart that stands firm for God. For it is clearer than day that since our adversaries are not clothed in human flesh, they cannot give as an excuse for their inability to overcome us that they are unable to enter us because we have closed the door against them. If they had been connected to this fragile body, when the entrance was blocked, access would have been denied to them. But although, as we said, they are free from this burden and are able to penetrate what has been blocked up and to fly all through the air without hindrance, it is obvious that because of their weakness the body of the church remains unharmed. The evil thugs, together with their leader, the devil, whom the Savior in the Gospel calls a murderer and the father of lies, would never have been beaten despite our brave fight against them, if their power had not been taken away. If I am lying, why do you spare us, Satan, you who rush around everywhere? Why are you, who are not imprisoned anywhere, unable to undermine the steadfastness of those who lead a life of virtue and who fight against you? But perhaps you love us, we whom you attempt each day to destroy? Is it credible that you are the master of goodness, and that you help rather than harm those who are very good? And what can be so dear to you as to cause hurt, particularly to those who fight bravely against your evil deeds? Who possesses a heart so prone to cunning? Who tries to carry out such practiced wiles? We know that you are the foulest corpse; we know that we live as Christians and are safe when we clash with you because the Lord has deprived you of your strength. That is why you are pierced by your own darts, because your threats have no effect. But if we are deceived, why do you attack our faith with terrifying phantoms and enormous shapes? If possibility were connected to willingness, the will alone would be enough for you. For it is a characteristic of power not to need outside assistance to deceive but to accomplish what it desires by means of its own strength. But now when you attempt to deceive, using changes of shape as in a theater, you prove more clearly that your strength is exhausted. The true angel of the Lord does not need help from other sources. Surely he does not require applause. But because your strength is weak, everlasting destruction follows you.

30. "But someone may ask, 'Why did the devil destroy Job's family? Why did he completely destroy Job's belongings, knock down his walls to their foundations, and build one tomb for his numerous children? Why did he afflict Job with strange and dreadful sores?' Anyone who makes such an objection must listen to the other side of the argument. It was not the devil who was able to do this, but the Lord. The Lord grants power against us twice over, either for our glory, if he approves of us, or for our punishment, if we do wrong. In fact, anyone who objects ought to understand from this that the devil could have done nothing, not even against one person, if he had not received his power from the Lord, for no one begs someone else for something that is in his own power. But why do I mention Job, whom the devil was unable to overcome even when he had got hold of him? The devil did not exercise his own strength against Job's cattle or sheep without God's permission.

31. "My dearest friends, a pure life and fearless faith in God are powerful weapons against the demons. Believe me, for I have experience with this. Nighttime devotions and the prayers, fasting, and gentleness of those who live rightly, terrify

Satan. He is afraid of these devoted ones because of their voluntary poverty, their lack of vanity, their humility, their compassion, their control over anger, and particularly because of their pure love for Christ. That foulest serpent knows that it is at God's command that he lies beneath the footsteps of the just. For the Lord said, *I have given you authority to tread on snakes and scorpions, and over all the power of the enemy* (Luke 10:19).

32. "But if they pretend they have the gift of divination, too, and predict the arrival of some of the brothers, and if those whom they predicted would come do indeed arrive, even then you must not trust them, for they are liars. That is why they anticipated those who were on their way, so that you might believe them when they made their announcement and gain admittance to you when they deceived you. A Christian should definitely not think there is anything miraculous in this, since it is not only demons that are able to arrive before those who are on their way. Men who travel ahead with the speed of horses can also announce that others will soon arrive. They are not referring to things that have not yet begun to happen, for God alone knows about future events. When they see the beginning of some action, they run like thieves and claim knowledge of it among those who are ignorant of it. For how many do you think there are now who could, if they were to run as fast as a boy, reveal to people far away our meeting here and its conversation, before anyone here had reported it?

33. "This was how paganism started: By means of these prophets' tricks, people believed the oracles spoken by the demons at the shrines. But at the coming of our Lord Jesus Christ they were silenced and became speechless and lost those they held captive. Who, I ask, thinks that a doctor has divine

foreknowledge, when from his study of illnesses he gauges
the fevers of a raging soul by means of the light pressure of
his fingers on the veins' pulse? Who would venerate with
supreme honor a sailor who uses the stars of heaven to find a
way on his sea voyage? Who would not praise a farmer for his
experience, rather than sanctify him as a god, if he makes
predictions about the dry heat in summer or the amount of
rain or the cold in winter? But if we admit for a moment that
the demons do predict true things, tell me, what advantage is
there in knowing what is to come? Surely no one ever wins
praise for knowing these things or is punished for not knowing
them. The question of whether each individual prepares for
himself either torments or glory depends solely on whether
he disregards the rules of Scripture or carries them out. None
of us chose this way of life so as to have foreknowledge of the
future but so that, obeying the Lord's commands, we might
begin to be his friends rather than his servants.

34. "We must not worry about knowing what is to come but
about carrying out what we have been told to do. Nor should
we demand this as a reward for the ascetic life. Instead, we
ought to ask the Lord for victory over the devil. If anyone
should happen to acquire the skill of divination, let him have
a pure heart that will enable him to know the future. For I
believe that the soul that serves God, if it continues steadfast
in its original purity, can know more than the demons. Such
was the soul of Elisha who witnessed powers unknown to
others.

35. "Now I will reveal to you other means of deception that the
demons practice. They often come at night, pretending to be
angels of God and praising the monks' dedication, admiring
their perseverance and promising future rewards. When you
see them, protect yourselves and your dwellings with the sign

of the cross, and they will dissolve immediately into nothing. For they fear that sign of victory by which the Savior, depriving them of their powers of the air, has shown them up. They also often leap around, twisting their limbs in contortions and show themselves to us to fill us with terror and horror. In this case, a firm faith in God will put them to flight as if they were merely feeble jokes. It is not difficult, with God's help, to distinguish between good and bad spirits. The holy angels are friendly and calm in appearance because they do not fight, nor will they cry out, nor will anyone hear their voice. In fact, they hurry on silently and smoothly, instilling joy, exultation, and confidence in men's hearts, seeing that the Lord is with them, he who is the source of happiness. Then our mind is no longer disturbed but becomes gentle and calm, illuminated by the angels' light; then the soul, aflame with desire for heavenly rewards, breaks out, if it is able, from its dwelling in the human body. Released from the burden of mortal limbs, it hastens toward heaven together with those whom it sees departing. Their kindness is so great that if anyone, due to human weakness, were terrified by their startling brightness, they would immediately dispel all fear from his heart. This was the case with Gabriel when he spoke to Zacharias in the temple, as with the angels who announced to the shepherds that Mary had given birth to Jesus. These angels revealed themselves to the untroubled minds of those who saw them; they told them that they should not be afraid. For fear is not so much a product of mental terror. It is often caused by the sight of mighty beings.

36. "The ferocious expressions of these most wicked creatures, along with their terrifying sounds and vile thoughts, immediately strike fear into the soul and numb the senses, producing nostalgia for family, fear of death, desire for sin, lack of

enthusiasm for virtue, and dullness of heart. If then joy and confidence in God's ineffable love replace this horror and trembling, we know that help has arrived, because calmness of the soul is proof of the presence of the holy power. This is why Abraham rejoiced when he saw God.

37. "But if the fear remains, the enemy has appeared, since he does not know how to comfort as Gabriel did when he told Mary not to be afraid. In fact, he increases fear and drives people right down into the deep pit of impiety to make them bow down before him. That is why the miserable pagans, unaware of the Lord's prohibition, mistakenly believed that the demons were gods. But the Lord did not allow the Christian peoples to be ensnared in these deceptions. He boldly repelled the devil in the Gospel when the devil claimed dominion over everything. The Lord said to him, *Away with you, Satan! for it is written, 'Worship the Lord your God, and serve only him'* (Matthew 4:10). The power conveyed by these words has been granted to us, too, for the Lord spoke like this so that apparent temptations should be shattered by the words of our Maker.

38. "I also advise you, my dearest friends, to be more concerned about your way of life than about miracles. If any of you performs miracles, he must neither swell with pride nor look down on those who cannot manage to perform them. Think about each individual's behavior. In this life it is proper for you to imitate what is perfect and to supply what is lacking. It is not for our humble selves to perform miracles but for the power of the Lord, who in the Gospel said to the disciples when they were boasting, *Do not rejoice that the spirits submit to you but rejoice that your names are written in heaven* (Luke 10:20). For the writing of names in the book of life is a testimony to virtue and merit, but the expulsion of Satan is a gift from the

Savior. That is why to those who take pride in prophetic signs rather than in the austerities of this life, and who say: *Did we not cast out demons in your name, and do many deeds of power in you name?* The Lord will reply: *I never knew you; go away from me, you evildoers* (Matthew 7:22–23). For the Lord does not know the ways of the ungodly. Let us therefore beg to deserve to receive the gift of distinguishing between spirits so that, in the words of Scripture, we may not trust every spirit.

39. "I had wished to finish talking now and to be silent regarding things that have happened to my humble self. But in case you should think that I have wasted my time mentioning things that could not possibly happen, I will tell you a few of the many things that have happened. Even if I am made to look foolish, yet the Lord who sees deep into my mind knows that I am doing this not out of a desire to boast but for the sake of your progress. How many times have the demons tried to make me proud by praising me excessively, although they received curses from me in the Lord's name? How many times did they threaten me with scorpions, huge beasts, and snakes that filled the house where I was living? But I countered by singing: *Some take pride in chariots, and some in horses, but our pride is in the name of the LORD our God* (Psalm 20:7). At once Christ's compassion put them to flight. On one occasion they appeared with a great light and said, 'Antony, we have come to bestow our brightness on you.' But I closed my eyes because I refused to look upon the devil's light. I prayed, and when I opened my eyes, the light of those wicked creatures had gone out. A few months later, when they were singing in front of me and quoting to each other from the Scriptures, I pretended I was deaf and did not listen. Sometimes they shook my prayer chamber, but I prayed to the Lord, my mind unmoved. Often they made loud noises, often they pranced

around me, and often they produced hissing sounds, but I sang psalms, and then the demons' sounds were turned to wailings.

40. "Do you believe, my sons, what I am telling you? Once I saw the devil standing very tall. He dared to claim that he was the power and providence of God, and he said to me, 'What do you want me to give you, Antony?' But I spat hard in his face and attacked him, protecting my entire self against him with the name of Christ. At once this tall figure of his disappeared just as I was about to get hold of him. While I was fasting he appeared to me as a monk and offered me bread, trying to persuade me in the following words to indulge this poor body of mine a little, 'You, too, are human,' he said, 'and limited by human weakness. Cease your efforts for a while, otherwise illness may snatch you away.' At once I recognized that serpent's ghastly face, and when I sought refuge as usual in the protection of Christ, he vanished like smoke wafting through an open window. In the desert he frequently tried to trap me with gold or to defile me by making me touch it. While I was being thrashed (for I was often beaten by the demons), I would chant words such as these: *Who will separate us from the love of Christ?* (Romans 8:35). When they heard this, the demons turned on one another in their rage and were put to flight, not at my command but at the Lord's, who said, *I watched Satan fall from heaven like a flash of lightning* (Luke 10:18). And so, my children, be mindful of Paul's words, *I have applied all these things to myself* (1 Corinthians 4:6), so that neither fear of demons nor any weariness might weaken your commitment to this way of life.

41. "Since I have made a fool of myself by recalling many things for your benefit, I also want to tell you something I experienced, and nobody who hears this can doubt that it is true.

Once a demon knocked on the door of my prayer chamber. When I went out I saw an enormously tall man. I asked him who he was, and he replied, 'I am Satan.' I asked him, 'What do you want here?' He answered, 'Why do the monks make false accusations against me? Why do all the Christian people curse me?' I said, 'They are right to accuse you, for your deceitful tricks often upset them.' But he answered, 'I do not do anything; it is they who cause each other trouble. Rather, I am to be pitied. I ask you, haven't you read: *The enemies have vanished in everlasting ruins?* (Psalm 9:6). Look, I have no place to be now; I possess no city; I have no weapons now. Throughout every nation and all the cities the name of Christ rings out, and even the desert is crammed full of monks. I beg you, let them look after themselves, and don't let them abuse me without any reason.' Then I marveled and rejoiced at God's grace and said to the demon these words: 'I cannot attribute such a strange and unheard-of idea to your truth, which is non-existent. For although you are the master of deceit, you have been forced to admit this without lying. Truly Jesus has utterly destroyed your powers; stripped of your honors as an angel, you lie rolling in the mud.' I had hardly finished speaking when his tall figure collapsed at the mention of the Savior's name.

42. "What room for hesitation can now remain, my children? What fear can there be any longer? What whirlwind of theirs could snatch us away? The soul of each individual should now feel secure. Don't let idle thoughts imagine dangers that don't exist. No one should fear that he will be carried off by the devil and dropped down a steep cliff. May all anxiety be dispelled, for the Lord, who has destroyed our enemies, remains in us as he promised, and has protected us from all of Satan's various attacks. Look how the devil himself, who tries

with his followers to practice deceit of this kind, admits that he can do nothing against Christians. Now, Christians and monks ought to be concerned in case their idleness gives the demons power. For the way they present themselves to us usually depends on the state in which they find us and our thoughts. If they find in our hearts some seed of dissatisfaction and fear, they pile up more fears and punish the unfortunate soul by making cruel threats. But if we are eager in the Lord and are inspired by a desire for future rewards and entrust everything to the Lord, no demon will be able to come close and try to surprise us. Instead, when the demons see that our hearts are fortified in Christ, they turn back in confusion. Thus the devil ran away from Job, who was strengthened in the Lord. But he robbed Judas of his faith and shackled him with the chains of captivity. There is, then, only one means of overcoming the enemy: spiritual joy and the constant recollection of a soul that is always thinking of the Lord. The soul that drives out the demons' tricks like smoke will attack its adversaries instead of fearing them. For Satan is well aware of the fires to come and knows of the huge fire blazing in hell.

43. "But to bring my speech to a conclusion, I will just mention one final thing. When a vision appears to you, demand boldly of it who it is and where it comes from. If it is a holy apparition, the angel's comfort will immediately turn your fear into joy. But if it is really a temptation offered by the devil, it will vanish when the faithful soul interrogates him. To ask who he is and where he is from offers the best guarantee of safety. In this way Joshua recognized the one who was helping him by questioning him, and the enemy, when he was questioned, was unable to hide from Daniel."

44. When Antony had finished speaking, everyone was in a joyful

mood. A desire for virtue flared up in some people. Flagging faith revived in others. False opinions were driven from the minds of some while groundless fears were driven out from others. At the same time, now that they felt contempt for the demons' insidious attacks, they all marveled at the great gift that the Lord had given Antony for distinguishing between spirits. And so there were on the mountain monastic prayer chambers like tents, filled with divine choirs of people singing psalms, reading, and praying. Antony's speech had inspired them all with such an eagerness to fast and to stay awake to pray that in their desire for the future fulfillment of their hope, they devoted themselves to showing mutual love and compassion for those in need. They appeared to inhabit an infinitely large area, a town removed from worldly matters, full of piety and justice. Anyone who set eyes on that multitude of ascetics, anyone who saw that heroic and harmonious community where no one caused any harm, where there was no slander, but a crowd of people leading lives of restraint, competing with each other in the performance of their duties, would immediately burst out with these words: *How fair are your tents, O Jacob, your encampments, O Israel! Like palm trees that stretch far away, like gardens beside a river, like aloes that the* LORD *has planted, like cedar trees beside the waters* (Numbers 24:5–6).

45. While these things were happening, causing the monks' commitment to a life of blessedness to increase each day, Antony was remembering the mansions set in heaven. He rejected the pointlessness of the present life, as if what he had already achieved was of little value, and established himself at a distance from the other brothers. When his human condition forced him to allow his poor body some food or sleep or any other necessities of nature, he was overcome by an extraordinary sense of shame, because the physical limitations

of his poor body restricted his spiritual freedom. For it often happened that while sitting with the brothers, he would think of his spiritual food and withdraw the meal set before him. Being human, however, he would eat, sometimes by himself, sometimes with the brothers. And while he acted in this strange way, he would persuade them with some embarrassment that great care must be shown, for the body must not be completely starved nor should it be overfed in case it should lose its ability to work, contrary to the Creator's will. For that reason every care must be taken to prevent the soul from succumbing to bodily vices and being pushed into hell's everlasting darkness. Instead, the soul should claim the authority granted to it in the flesh and raise its dwelling up to the third heaven, like the apostle Paul. Antony claimed that this was what the Savior meant when he said: *Do not worry, saying "What will we eat?" or "What will we drink?" or "What will we wear?" for your heavenly father knows that you need all these things. But strive first for the kingdom of God and his righteousness, and all these things will be given to you as well* (Matthew 6:31–33).

46. After these events, when cruel persecution was raging out of control and devastating the church, Antony left his prayer chamber to follow those who were to become martyrs for Christ, saying, "Let us go and be present at the glorious triumph of our brothers. We shall either take part in the fight ourselves, or we shall watch the others in battle." In his love he was already a martyr, but since he could not give himself up of his own accord and he was ministering to the confessors in the mines and prisons, he exhorted with great concern those entering the law court. He hoped to prevent them from being driven to deny Christ because of their fear of wicked persecutors. Rejoicing that the sentence given meant that they would receive the martyr's crown, as if he himself were the

victor he accompanied them as far as the place where their blessed blood was to be shed. The judge was disturbed by Antony and his friends' steadfastness, and he gave the order that no monk should watch the trial or stay in the city. And on that day everyone else thought it a good idea to hide. But Antony had no fear. He disregarded the prosecutor's order and washed his coat. The next day he took up a prominent position, dressed in white, to catch the judge's attention as he walked past. Antony was burning with desire for martyrdom. He demonstrated to us that Christians ought to persist in an attitude that scorns punishment and death. He was saddened by the fact that despite his wish to suffer for the name of God, he was not granted martyrdom. But the Lord, who was preparing a leader for his flock, saved Antony so that the monastic way of life would be strengthened not only by his words but also by his example. And yet he always followed so closely in the footsteps of the martyrs that, bound by anxious concern for them and by the bonds of love, he suffered more than they did from imprisonment, even though he was locked out.

47. But when the persecution died away, and the blessed bishop Peter had been crowned with a martyr's glory, Antony returned to his former prayer chamber and achieved a daily martyrdom of faith and conscience, wearing himself out by means of more rigorous fasting and nightly devotions. He wore a hair shirt next to his skin and a garment of animal skin on top. He never washed his body and never wiped the dirt from his feet, except when necessity compelled him to cross through water. In fact, no one saw Antony's body naked until his death.

48. At one time, when Antony had withdrawn from everyone's eye and had closed his prayer chamber, refusing to receive

visitors, a military officer, whose daughter was possessed with an evil spirit, knocked at his door. He begged Antony to help his dear child and to come out and pray to God for his daughter. Antony had not the slightest desire to open the door, but he looked down from above and said, "Why do you ask me for help, you who are a mortal man? I, too, am mortal and share your weakness. But if you believe in Christ, whose servant I am, go and pray to God according to your faith, and your daughter will be healed." Immediately the officer believed and went away. When he had called on Jesus, his daughter was restored to health, and he took her home. The Lord also worked many other miracles through Antony. For the one who promised in the Gospel, *Ask and it will be given to you* (Matthew 7:7), did not deny his power to the man he found so worthy to receive it. For many suffering people came and slept in front of the closed entrance to Antony's prayer chamber and were cured through him by means of their faithful prayers to Christ.

49. However, the arrival of so many people was a nuisance to him, for they deprived him of the solitude he desired. As a result, he feared that the miracles granted to him might either make him proud or induce others to have a higher estimate of him than he deserved. Antony decided to go to another place where he was not so well known. When the brothers had given him some bread, he sat on the bank of the river, watching for a boat to come by. As he sat there, a voice came to him from above, saying, "Antony, where are you going, and why?" He answered, "Since the people do not leave me in peace, I thought it would be best for me to move on, especially since their demands often exceed my power." The voice said to him, "If you move to this other place, your burden will be twice as heavy as the one you now carry. But if you really

want to live in peace, go even further into the desert." When Antony asked, "Who can show me that remote place, for I do not know the area?" The speaker immediately pointed out some travelers. Antony approached them and asked them to take him with them into the desert. Since no one had any objection, they welcomed his company as if God had sent him. After a journey of three days and nights, he came to a high mountain, at the foot of which there flowed a stream of sweet water. On a small strip of flat land around the mountain a few untended palm trees grew.

50. Antony fell in love with this spot, as God had offered it to him. He accepted some bread from his fellow travelers, and he remained alone on the mountain, without any companion. He lived there as if he recognized this place as his own home. His fellow travelers, seeing his joyful determination, chose to travel that way often to visit him. They happily brought loaves of bread to him, for the palm trees sustained him only slightly.

51. Later, when the brothers discovered where he was, they sent him food, much like sons taking care of their fathers. Then Antony realized that for the sake of his comfort, many were being asked to perform burdensome tasks. Wishing to spare the monks these burdens, he asked those who were coming to see him to bring him a hoe and some seeds. When he received these, he searched around his home and found an area where he could plant the seeds. He used the mountain spring to irrigate his garden plot. When he had planted his seeds, they produced a crop of wheat large enough for a year's supply of bread. He was pleased to live in the desert by the work of his own hands, without troubling anyone else. But when some people again began to arrive there, he took pity on their exhaustion and grew vegetables in a small garden, so the visitors could be restored when they arrived

after their difficult journey. But the animals that came there to drink the water ate the small crop intended for the monks' refreshment. Catching hold of one of them, Antony said to them all, "Why do you harm me when I have done you no harm? Go away, and in the Lord's name do not come near here any more." Who would believe that as a result of this command the animals, as if they were afraid, never came near the place?

52. When Antony took possession of the mountainous areas and the interior regions of the desert in this way, devoting himself to prayer, the brothers who came to see him could only with difficulty persuade him to agree to accept olives and oil and to make some concessions to his old age. It was shocking to see what terrible struggles he went through while he was living there. Indeed, we learned from those who visited him that his *struggle was not against enemies of flesh and blood but against the cosmic powers of this present darkness, against the spiritual forces of evil in the heavenly places* (cf. Ephesians 6:12). For they reported hearing loud noises, people's voices, and the clash of weapons. They said they saw the mountains filled with hordes of demons, while Antony stood firm and bravely wrestled with them. But he also comforted and encouraged his visitors. At the same time, he destroyed the entire army of Satan, using prayers as his weapons. It is certainly remarkable that one man, living in such great solitude, should not have been terrified out of his wits by these daily clashes with the demons. Rightly David sang: *Those who trust in the Lord are like Mount Zion* (Psalm 125:1). Antony kept his resolve, calm and unshaken. In this way he managed to put the demons to flight and to make the wild beasts be at peace with him.

53. But the devil gnashed his teeth as he watched Antony. With the Savior's help, Antony remained safe from all attacks. One

night when Antony was staying awake to pray to the Lord, the devil gathered so many packs of wild animals outside his prayer chamber that Antony saw that all the creatures of the desert surrounded him. When they snarled at him, threatening to tear his body with their teeth, he understood the enemy's cunning. So he said, "If the Lord has given you permission to attack me, I will let you devour me. But if you are sent here by demons, go away as fast as you can, for I am one of Christ's servants." When they heard his command, all the beasts ran away as if the lash of God's power had whipped them.

54. A few days later another struggle took place with the same enemy. Antony was always busy working so he could present visitors with some small gift to repay them for the things they brought him. One day when he was weaving a basket, something pulled one of the reeds out of the basket. This made Antony stand up, and he saw a creature whose upper body had a human form but whose lower body was like a donkey's. Seeing this, Antony made the sign of the cross on his own forehead and said, "I am one of Christ's servants: If you have been sent to me, I will not run away." There was not a moment's delay. At once the hideous monster fled with its attendant evil spirits, and as it rushed away it was destroyed. The death of the monster marked the destruction of all the demons that, in spite of their efforts, were unable to drive Antony out of the desert. These marvelous deeds were followed by many more.

55. Not long after these events Antony went out and was forced to yield to the brothers' pleas to come and visit them. After packing a supply of bread and water, he set off with them. About halfway along their journey, their water supply ran out. The excessive blazing of the sun and the unbearable heat

threatened to kill them. They searched for at least a pool of rainwater, but did not find any relief that would save them. Even the camel looked as if it were about to die of thirst. The old man was moved by the danger staring them all in the face, and in his distress he sighed deeply. Taking refuge in prayer, he withdrew from them for a short while. He knelt down and stretched out his hands in prayer to the Lord. As soon as the tears fell from his eyes, a bubbling spring burst forth in the exact spot where he was praying. When they had quenched their thirst and cooled their burning arms, they filled their water containers and then let the camel drink. At last, Antony came to the monks who had invited him. They all ran to meet him as if he were their father, competing with each other in their eagerness to greet him respectfully with kisses and hugs. Antony was happy to see how fervently they practiced their commitment to the monastic way of life. They were all happy at his arrival, for he brought gifts of spiritual nourishment. He praised the rigorous self-discipline of the old monks and encouraged the new ones. When he saw his sister, who had grown old as a virgin and was now in charge of other girls, he embraced her joyfully. Then he hurried back to the mountain, as if he had been away from the desert for a long time.

56. There now came to him many people troubled by demons. He consoled these people, while he gave the same message to all the monks, saying, "Have faith in Jesus; keep your mind free from wicked thoughts and your body free from all filthiness. In accordance with the divine sayings, do not be seduced by a full stomach. Detest pride, pray frequently, recite the psalms in the evening, in the morning, and at noon, and meditate on the Scripture's commands. Remember the deeds of the saints so that their example will inspire your soul

to virtue and restrain it from vice." He also used to persuade them constantly to bear in mind Paul's words: *Do not let the sun go down on your anger* (Ephesians 4:26). Antony interpreted this as meaning that the sun should set not only upon anger but also upon any human sin. He also warned us to remember Paul's commandment to *examine yourselves and test yourselves* (cf. 2 Corinthians 13:5). By keeping a close watch, they could refrain from sinning if they discovered any sin in themselves. If they did not find any error, they could stand firm in their commitment to the monastic life. But they should not become proud or contemptuous of others or claim a special righteousness for themselves. Many are the ways that seem just to men, but they end with a view into the depths of hell. Often we cannot see our own sins, and we are deceived by ignorance of our own deeds. God judges not on outward appearances but according to the secrets of the mind. It is right for us to show compassion to one another and to bear one another's burdens. By leaving judgment to the Savior, we can keep watch on our own consciences by examining ourselves. Antony also used to say that the path to virtue is a wide one if each person were either to watch what he was doing or to report all his thoughts to the brothers. For no one can sin when he has to report all his sins to someone else and endure the shame of revealing his wicked deeds in public. No sinner dares to sin in front of someone else. Even if he does sin, he wants to avoid a witness to his sin and prefers to lie and deny it, thus increasing his error by adding the error of denial. "And so," Antony used to say, "we are put to shame if we do everything with a view to giving a report of it, but much more so if we write down our sins in an orderly fashion, describing them faithfully. Then the account of our sins will be set clearly before the brothers' eyes. If we fear that the wax tablets will know of our sins, the letters themselves prove our guilt. And just as those who have sex with prostitutes are embarrassed by others' presence, so we too blush at the writing, if we do this. Let us walk this path of virtue, and, keeping our bodies under the mind's control, let us destroy the devil's destructive plans."

57. With encouraging words like these he inspired those monks who came to him to pursue their life of rigorous self-discipline, and he sympathized with those who were suffering. Through Antony the Lord freed many of them from their sufferings. He never became arrogant because he succeeded in healing so many people, nor did he become depressed because some of the bodies still were possessed by demons. Instead he gave thanks to God, always maintaining the same attitude and the same look. He persuaded those who were possessed to bear with great patience the attacks tormenting them. "For this medicine does not belong to me or to any other human being but to God alone. God grants healing to those he chooses and at the time he chooses." And so by means of his advice he taught those who were tormented to bear their trials with patience. He taught those who had already been freed, to give thanks to God, not to Antony.

58. A man tormented by violent demons—they caused him to cut his tongue with his teeth and tried to blind him—arrived at the mountain and asked the blessed old man to pray to the Lord on his behalf. Antony prayed and said to the man, "Go, you will be healed." But the man did not believe this, violently refusing to listen to Antony. So Antony repeated the same message to him, saying, "You cannot be cured here. Go away, and when you reach a certain place, Christ's mercy will come upon you immediately." At last the man was persuaded and set off. As soon as he reached that certain place, the devil's

possession ceased, just as Antony had promised in accordance with the Lord's revelation to him while he prayed.

59. There was a young girl suffering from an unknown disease. Her suffering was increased by the fact that her body was paralyzed and that she was unnaturally cross-eyed. When her parents heard that the monks were going to Antony, they took her to him. For they had faith in the Lord, who in the Gospel had commanded the hemorrhage to stop when the woman touched the hem of his tunic. The parents asked the monks to let their poor daughter accompany them, but the monks refused. So the parents carried her to Antony and waited outside with their sick daughter. They waited in the company of the blessed confessor and monk Paphnutius, who had been blinded and disfigured for his faith. When the monks came to Antony and began to tell him about the girl's illness, the old man anticipated their account and related the entire story of her illness and her journey, as if he himself had been there. When the monks asked him to permit the parents to enter with their daughter, Antony would not allow it. Instead, he said, "Go, and you will find the girl healed, if she is not dead. No one should come to me, insignificant creature that I am, for the bestowal of cures is not a matter for human wretchedness, but for the mercy of Jesus Christ, who always gives assistance to those who believe in him wherever they are. That is why this girl, too, for whom you ask my help, has been released as a result of her own prayers. When I prayed to the Lord, I was granted foreknowledge of her cure." He spoke, and his words were followed by the girl's restoration to health. When the monks went out, they found the girl healthy and her parents overjoyed.

60. A few days later when two brothers were traveling to see Antony, their water supply ran out. One of them died of

thirst, while the other lay on the ground waiting to die. Antony, who was on the mountain, quickly called to two monks and told them to grab a bottle of water and to hurry along the route where the travelers were lying. He told them, "One of the brothers who is on his way here has just passed away to the Lord; the other will do so, too, unless you help him. This was revealed to me just now as I was praying." The monks hurried off. They found the dead body and covered it with earth. They revived the other monk and carried him back. Perhaps someone may ask, "Why did Antony not speak before the monk died?" But this question is utterly inappropriate for Christians to ask, because the judgment did not come from Antony but from God, who passed the sentence he wished on the dying man and who was kind enough to give a revelation about the thirsty man. The remarkable thing is that Antony, who was living on a mountain far away, became aware of everything happening at a great distance, because the Lord made it known to his ever-watchful heart.

61. On another occasion while he was living on the mountain, Antony suddenly raised his eyes to the sky and saw something that appeared to be a soul moving toward heaven, while angels rejoiced at its approach. He was amazed at this strange sight. Blessing the choir of holy beings, he prayed that some understanding of this matter might be revealed to him. Immediately there came to him a voice saying that this was the soul of the monk Ammon. Ammon was a very old man who had continued in a life of holiness from childhood to old age. When the monks saw Antony in a state of wonder, they asked him to explain the cause of his joy. He told them that Ammon, whom they knew very well because of his visits to Antony and because of his famous miracles, had just died. The monks whom Antony had told about Ammon's death

made a note of the day. When the brothers from Ammon's prayer chamber came to visit, the monks asked them about Ammon's death and found that he had died on the very day and at the very hour the old man had seen his soul being carried to heaven. They were amazed at the purity of Antony's mind, in that the knowledge of something happening so far away—Ammon's prayer chamber was a thirteen-day trip for Antony—had reached him without delay.

62. When a certain man found Antony at the Outer Mountain, he asked him to pray for Polycratia, a virgin whose dedication to Christ was remarkable. She was suffering from the most terrible pains in her stomach and her side. As a result of excessive fasting and lack of sleep, her body was completely worn out. Antony prayed, and the man made a note of the day on which the prayer had been made. Then he returned and found the virgin healed. When he asked her on which day she had been cured, he found that the time of healing corresponded to the time of Antony's prayer. Everyone was amazed, for they realized that the Lord had released her from her pains at the moment when Antony, in his prayer for her, was appealing to the Savior's goodness.

63. He also often foretold, days and months in advance, the times of arrival of the many people who came to him, as well as their reason for coming. For some were drawn there by their great desire to see him, others by illness, and some because their body was possessed by demons. But no one ever complained of any trouble or loss resulting from the difficult journey, and they all went home filled with spiritual food. But Antony used to tell them that they should not praise him for this marvel. Rather they should praise the Lord, who grants knowledge of himself to men according to their human capacity.

64. On one occasion he went out to the outer prayer chambers and was asked by the brothers to pray in a boat with some monks who were setting off. He climbed on board and was the only one among them to notice a most revolting smell. Everyone assured him that it was the stink of the salted and pickled fish lying in the boat. But he told them he was sure he could smell the stench of something else. While he was still speaking, a young man in the grip of a demon, who had hidden himself in the boat, suddenly cried out. Antony immediately cured him in the name of our Lord Jesus Christ, and all the people realized that it was the devil that had given off that foul smell.

65. Another man possessed with an evil spirit was brought to Antony. He was afflicted with such a degree of madness that he did not realize he was in Antony's presence, and he was even eating his own feces. When the old man was asked to pray to the Lord for him, he felt such compassion for the young man's wretched state that he stayed awake all night with him, striving to overcome the sufferer's madness. When dawn came, the possessed man attacked Antony and gave him a hard push. Those who had brought him there became angry and began to ask him why he had hurt the old man. But Antony said to them, "Do not blame the poor young man. The one who possesses him causes this madness. The enemy, who was offended because the Lord ordered him to come to this dry region, attacked me in this presumptuous way. This attack on me was a sign that Satan had been driven out." No sooner had Antony spoken than the young man returned to his senses and gave thanks to God. He now recognized where he was. Filled with love, the young man hugged Antony and kissed him.

66. There are countless other miracles like this about which we
    have learned from the monks' frequent accounts. But we
    should not be as amazed by these as by the following ones
    that far exceed the weakness of our human condition. Once,
    when Antony had begun to pray before a meal, he felt him-
    self being caught up in the spirit and being carried on high
    by angels. But when the demons prevented them from passing
    through the air, the angels began to ask their opponents why
    they would hold Antony back, since he had no faults. The
    demons tried to set forth his sins, going back to the time of
    his birth, but the angels shut the demons' slanderous mouths,
    saying that they should not recount his sins from birth. For
    Antony's sins had already been laid to rest through Christ's
    goodness. But if they knew of any from the period after he
    had become a monk and devoted himself to God, they might
    mention those. The demons, lying shamelessly, accused him
    of many things. But since they could not prove their lies,
    Antony's way up to heaven lay open and unobstructed.
    Immediately returning to himself, he saw himself as he had
    been, in the very place where he had been standing. Then he
    forgot all about his meal. From that hour he spent the entire
    night lamenting, reflecting on the great number of enemies
    that humans have and on their difficult journey through the
    air to heaven. He remembered Paul's saying that *our struggle is
    not against flesh and blood but against the prince of the power of the air*
    (cf. Ephesians 6:12). Paul knew that the powers of the air are
    always trying, by wrestling and fighting, to prevent us from
    gaining an unobstructed passage to heaven. So Paul encour-
    aged us with this advice: *Put on the whole armor of God* (Ephesians
    6:11), so that *any opponent will have nothing evil to say of us* (Titus
    2:8). Let us remember Paul's words: *Whether in the body or out of
    the body, I do not know; God knows* (2 Corinthians 12:2). And in

fact Paul was swept up as far as the third heaven. After Paul had heard words there that cannot be spoken on earth, he came down again. Antony, though, was raised right up to the heavens, and after his struggles he appeared unhindered.

67. Antony also possessed the following kind of gift: If there were something he did not know and if he were wondering about it, the Lord would reveal it to him as he prayed. As it says in the Scripture, God taught him. Later, the brothers were holding a discussion and were earnestly questioning him about what happened to the soul after the body had died and where the soul was allowed to go after death. The following night they heard a voice from on high calling his name. It said, "Antony, get up. Go and look outside." So he got up and went out. Raising his eyes to heaven, he saw someone tall and terrifying, his head reaching as far as the clouds. He also saw some winged creatures trying to fly up to heaven, but the tall being stretched out his arms to prevent them from getting through. The tall being caught some of these creatures and threw them back to the ground. Others he tried unsuccessfully to hold back, and he seemed annoyed when they managed to fly past him up toward heaven. Those who got the better of him caused him grief, but those who were beaten back gave him the greatest joy. At once a voice came to Antony saying, "Pay attention to what you see." Then his heart was illuminated and he began to understand that these were souls that the devil was blocking in their ascent. He realized that the devil took hold of those who were subject to him, but he was tormented by the flight of the holy ones whom he was unable to catch. Inspired by the examples offered in these visions, Antony advanced each day to better things. He did not tell the brothers what had been

revealed to him, for he did not wish to boast. But since he praised God constantly in his prayers for God's assistance, he was forced to explain these things to the brothers whenever they asked. He did not want to conceal anything from his spiritual sons, for his soul was pure in Christ, especially since the recounting of miracles like this one was likely to stimulate their passion for that way of life and show them what the fruit of their labors might produce.

68. Antony was never provoked to impatience by sudden anger. He did not allow his humility to become puffed up into pride. He urged all the clerics, right down to the lowest rank, to pray before he did. He also bent his head for the bishops and the priests to give him their blessing, as if he were their disciple in humility. Even when deacons came to him for their own benefit, he would speak to them in order to help them. When it came to praying to the Lord, he put them before himself, for he was not ashamed to learn from them. In fact, he frequently questioned those who were with him. If they told him something useful, he admitted that they had helped him. His face bore a look of exceptional grace, and he also possessed a wonderful gift from the Savior. If anyone who did not know him wanted to see him when he was surrounded by a large number of monks, he would go past all the others and run up to Antony without having anyone to point him out. He could recognize Antony's spiritual purity from his face, and through the mirror of Antony's body he would perceive the grace of his holy mind. For Antony always had a cheerful look that showed that his mind was on heavenly matters. As it says in Scripture: *A glad heart makes a cheerful countenance, but by sorrow of heart the spirit is broken* (Proverbs 15:13). This was how Jacob recognized that Laban, his uncle, was devising some

plot against him, and so he said to his wives: *Your father does not regard me as favorably as he did before* (Genesis 31:5). This was how Samuel recognized David, for he had eyes that brought joy, and teeth as white as milk. In the same way, people recognized Antony, because he always kept the same expression in good times and bad. He was neither elated by his successes nor shattered by his disasters. For his face made people love him, and the purity of his faith made them marvel at him.

69. He never associated with the schismatic party, because he was aware of their long-standing wickedness and apostasy. He never went so far as to bestow friendly words on the Manicheans or other heretics, except such words that alone might call them back from the error of their ways. He spoke out against friendship with them, and he denounced what they said, believing that such teachings lead to spiritual ruin. He detested the Arians, too, warning everyone not to go anywhere near them. When some of the Arians came to him, he questioned them carefully and found that their sect was utterly sacrilegious. So he sent them away from the mountain, saying their words were far more poisonous than serpents.

70. Once when the Arians falsely claimed that Antony held the same beliefs as they did, he was amazed at their audacity and was moved to righteous indignation. Antony publicly condemned the Arians, declaring that this was the final heresy that would herald the arrival of the Antichrist. He stated openly to the people that the Son of God is not a creature; he was not brought into existence out of non-being, but is eternal, of one substance with the Father. He must not be regarded as something created or adopted, or as a mere name. He said that it was sacrilegious to say that there was a time when he was not, since the Word of God, who is eternal, is coeternal with the Father, for he was born from the Father

who exists forever. And so he used to say, "You must have nothing to do with the Arians. *What fellowship is there between light and darkness?* (2 Corinthians 6:14). You who hold orthodox beliefs are Christians. But the Arians teach that the Son who comes from God the Father is a creature. So they are no different from the pagans who worship the creature instead of the Creator, who is blessed forever. Believe me, the entire creation groans in the face of the Arians' madness, because it sees its Lord, through whom and in whom all things were made, being numbered among the creatures."

71. It is impossible to convey the degree to which this great man's words strengthened the people's faith. They rejoiced that a pillar of the church was condemning this dangerous heresy, hostile to Christ. At that time no one, of any age or of either sex, remained at home. I am not speaking just of the Christians. Even the pagans and the priests of the idols came rushing to church, saying, "We beg to see the man of God." They crowded around him, eager just to touch the hem of his garment, because they believed that merely touching it would benefit them greatly. How many people were freed from the devil's grip and from many different illnesses at that time! How many spoils were snatched from the idols! How many people were retrieved from pagan error and added to our flock! The number of those converted from the superstition of the idols in the space of a few days would no doubt be greater than the number of converts one would normally see in a year. His attendants began to turn the crowd away, because they thought that he would find this number of people a nuisance. He said calmly, "Surely this gathering is no larger than the hosts of demons? Surely this crowd of followers is no more numerous than the army of those with whom I wrestled on the mountain?"

72. While we were escorting him back, a woman called out from behind, saying, "Wait, man of God. My daughter is tormented by the most hideous demon. Wait, I beg you. Wait, for otherwise I may die in my hurry to reach you." On hearing this, the wonderful old man stopped for a while. When the woman came up to him, the girl was hurled to the ground and lay there while Antony prayed to the Lord Jesus. At his threats the unclean spirit departed immediately. The girl was restored to health; the people praised God, and the mother was overjoyed. Antony, too, was pleased because he was returning to the solitude he longed for.

73. He was also remarkably wise. Considering he had no education, it was amazing how very clever and shrewd he was. One time when he was at the Outer Mountain, two pagan philosophers came to see him, thinking they could outwit him. When he saw them, he knew from their appearance that they were pagan. Going out to them, he said to them through an interpreter: "Why did these men want to put themselves to the trouble of such a long journey to visit a stupid man?" When they said that he was not stupid but rather exceedingly wise, he replied pointedly, "If you have come to see a stupid man, your effort is wasted. But if you think I am wise and that I possess wisdom, it would be a good idea for you to imitate what you approve of, for it is right to imitate good things. If I had come to you, I would imitate you. But since you have come to me believing that I am wise, you should be Christians like me." The philosophers went away, amazed at his mental acuteness and at his ability to drive out demons.

74. He used these kinds of argument to check others, too, who were similarly full of worldly wisdom, people who wished to mock him because he was uneducated. He would say to such people, "What comes first, mind or letters? And which is the

cause of which? Does mind come from letters, or letters from the mind?" When they declared that mind was the author and inventor of letters, he said, "So, if anyone's mind is sound, he has no need of letters?" Was there anyone present who did not exclaim in astonishment after this verbal contest, when even those whom he got the better of were astounded, marveling at such great sagacity of mind in one who was uneducated? Even though he had spent his entire life living in the desert and the mountains, Antony was not boorish and lacking in grace. Rather, he was pleasant and friendly, and offered conversation that was seasoned with divine salt. No one felt any ill will toward him, and he gained the affection of all.

75. Meanwhile, for a third time men who were blinded by the fog of secular wisdom and who, in their own minds, were the most learned in all branches of philosophy came to visit Antony. When they demanded that Antony explain the Christian faith and tried to trick him by asking cunning questions about the divine cross, he remained silent and pitied their errors. Then he began to speak through an interpreter. He said, "What is more honorable, what is more proper—to worship the cross or to attribute adultery, parricide, or incest to those whom you worship? In the one case, contempt for death is a sign of virtue, but in the other a shameful religion is the teacher of obscenity. Is it better to say that the Word of God, remaining what he was, took a human body for the sake of our salvation, so that by sharing our human condition he might take us up to heaven, allowing us to share in the heavenly nature? Or is it better to claim, as you do, that the breath of the divine mind bows his head to worship earthly things and confines the heavenly name within the forms of cattle and serpents? How do you dare to mock the credulity of Christians because they claim that Christ, the Son of God,

without suffering any harm, began to be what he was not while remaining what he had been? You yourselves derive the soul from the heavenly beings but then envelop souls not only in human bodies but also in the bodies of serpents and cattle. Christian belief states that its God has come for the salvation of the world, but you, while proclaiming that the soul is unborn, change from one side to another. Christian faith, respecting God's omnipotence and mercy as it does, says that the Incarnation was possible for God, but in such a way that this condescension did not cause him to lose dignity. But you who claim proudly that the soul, issuing from the purest source of God, has fallen shamefully, and who dare to state that it is subject to change after its fall, you desecrate this nature, too, with your wicked tongues and insults to the soul. According to you, the image that retains the natural likeness of its Maker, who has the same substance as that which flows from it, consequently sends back its own humiliation and injuries to its origin. As a result of your blasphemy, your insults to the soul will reflect on their father, as you call him.

76. "At this point let us bring the cross of Christ, the Lord our God, into the argument. I ask, how is this an obscenity of religion? Isn't it better to endure the cross or a death of this kind inflicted by wicked men than to bewail the unsettled and dubious travels of Isis and Osiris? Don't the plots of Typhon, the flight of Saturn, and his most cruel devouring of his own children embarrass you? Blush at Jupiter's murder of his father; blush at the rape he committed, and his sexual acts with women and boys. These are what you believe; these are what you worship; these are the ornaments adorning your temples. Weigh your words with impartial justice for the sake of your salvation. Is all or nothing to be believed in Christian

books? If nothing, you should not acknowledge the name of the cross you belittle. If, on the hand, it is to be believed, why do you tear apart the divine passion with your stupid arguments, when in the same books the resurrection is connected to the cross? Why don't you also question the sight of the blind, the hearing of the deaf, the walking of the lame, the cleansing of the leprous, and the return from the underworld of those who were dead? All these things are included in the divine Scriptures, which you falsify. These same volumes contain the proclamations of divine power and the disgrace inflicted upon death. For this reason, put away your hatred, and you will discover immediately that Jesus is true God and that he took our weak nature upon himself for the sake of human salvation.

77. "Now tell us about your religion, if you are not ashamed to do so. But how could you mistaken ones call such disgraceful and foolish things religious practices? Unless you claim, as I have heard that you do, that the obscene and cruel behavior of your gods, their deceptions, and their deaths are but myths, and you interpret them allegorically. According to your interpretation, the rape of Libera represents the earth; the half-lame and weak Vulcan represents fire; Juno represents the air; Apollo, the sun; Diana, the moon; Neptune, the seas; Jupiter, the chief lecher, represents the sky. But after this bold attempt at a cover-up, you disregard the Creator and acknowledge the created things, not God. If the beauty of the elements has drawn you to worship them, you should have limited yourselves to admiring them and not worshiping them. For the worship of created things might imply an insult to the Creator. According to your distorted logic, the honor due to the architect is transferred to the building. The doctor's skill is attributed to the cures and the rewards. Praises

due to all craftsmen are bestowed instead on the products themselves. What do you say to this? We want to know what disgraceful belief you hold about the cross, which you consider worthy of ridicule."

78. This argument caused the philosophers to look around at one another and grumble. Then Antony smiled and spoke once again through the interpreter. "It seems very hard, in the case of any task, whenever a reasonable attitude to something is scorned and the reward for the task is bestowed on the deeds rather than the doers. Indeed, sight itself proves that the elements are in servitude. But since you are collecting all these things that are necessary for dialectical proof, you force us to use this ploy to affirm our religion. Please answer me: How is knowledge of God proved more clearly? By means of intricate arguments, or by the working of faith? And which comes first: the working of faith, or debate proceeding by means of arguments?" When they answered that the working of faith was more effective than discussion, and that this offered an accurate knowledge of God, he agreed that they had spoken well. For the working that derives from faith is produced by feelings in the mind, while dialectical argument depends on the skill of those setting it forth. "And so," he said, "anyone who has faith working in his mind will find unnecessary the composition of words that you use to try to tear out the credulity rooted in our minds. Yet often you are unable to explain what we understand. Therefore, the products of the mind are more reliable than the deceptive conclusions derived from philosophical arguments.

79. "We Christians keep the mystery of our life stored up, not in worldly wisdom, but in the power of faith that God has granted to us through Christ. The daily order of events proves the truth of what I say. For us, being ignorant and

lacking your learning, God's words are sufficient to attain the knowledge of God. Look at all of us, we who have been taken from pagan flocks. Each day we increase in number and are spreading throughout the entire world. It is undeniable that since the coming of the Lord your complicated philosophical arguments have failed you. Look at us, the ones who teach Christ's simple faith. We have completely crushed the worship of idols. The preaching of the cross, which is despised, has caused golden temples to collapse. Show us, if you can, those who have been persuaded by your intricate arguments to value paganism above Christ. Throughout the entire world Christ has now been acknowledged as the true Son of God. Sophisticated philosophical arguments cannot stop the growing number of believers. When we call on the name of the crucified one, all the demons roar. Yet you worship them as gods. As soon as the sign of the Lord's cross is made, they flee from the bodies in which they have been dwelling.

80. "Where are those legendary oracles now? What good did the magician's spells do? Everything was destroyed when Christ thundered forth to the world from his cross. Yet you fail to mention the throngs of those whose strength is broken. Instead you try to pour scorn on Jesus' glorious death. How is that paganism, so beloved by the world and never persecuted by tyrants, is now destroyed? In contrast, the more they try to suppress us—Christ's servants—the more we rise up and flourish. Decorated walls once surrounded your statues, but now the passing of time has caused them to collapse. Christ's teachings that appear so foolish and trivial to you are not restricted to any one area and are not confined within the boundaries of any barbarian peoples, in spite of the persecution of Christians. When did brightness as great as that of

divine knowledge shine forth? When did so many virtues appear at the same time? The martyrs' glorious commitment to their Lord shines forth, for the cross of Christ provides the foundation for all of their lives.

81. "In the midst of such great companies of virtues you try to blot out the true light with your obscure arguments. We don't use philosophical persuasion but the clearest faith, which always comes prior to verbal affirmation, to convince people of the true light. There are some here who are suffering from the demons' torments. Use any of your spells or philosophical arguments to drive out those whom you think of as your gods. But if you are unable to do so, hold out your conquered hands in prayer and take refuge in Christ's victory. The power of the divine majesty will immediately follow upon belief in the crucified one." He called on the name of Jesus and made the life-giving mark on their foreheads three times, corresponding to the number of the holy Trinity. As a result, the demons were driven out and the foolish wisdom of the philosophers was refuted. They were shocked and terrified by Antony, to whom God was granting such wisdom as well as the ability to perform miracles. But he attributed everything to Christ, who heals. He said, "Don't think I am the one who has given these people health. Christ performs these miracles through his servants. You, too, should believe, and you will see that it is devout faith in God, rather than empty pride and clever talk, that is rewarded by such miracles. Take refuge in the crucified one, and imitate us who are his servants. Content with this faith, don't seek further arguments based on worldly ignorance." Antony stopped speaking, and the amazed philosophers departed from him after saying a respectful farewell. They admitted to one another that their meeting with him had helped them greatly.

82. The remarkable thing about this man was that he who lived in obscurity on the farthest edge of the world found favor with the emperors and was honored by the imperial court. But Antony was not affected by such recognition. He showed no excitement at receiving greetings from emperors. He called the monks together and said, "The rulers of this world have sent us letters; why should Christians be impressed by this? For although we are different in rank, we are all humans. What should be honored with all due reverence, what should be held firmly and positively in mind, is that God wrote the law for all people and that he enriched the churches with his own words through his Son. What business do monks have with the letters of emperors? Why should I receive letters, to which I do not know how to reply with the customary formalities?" But when the brothers asked him to bring comfort to the Christian rulers by writing to them, he wrote a suitable reply to the letters he had received. First, he praised them for worshiping Christ, and then gave them advice about their salvation to keep them from thinking that imperial power was anything wonderful or allowing their authority to make them proud. He did not want them to forget that they were human and that they would have to be judged by Christ. Finally, he strongly advised them to show compassion and justice to those who were subject to them, and to show concern for the poor. In his letter he also declared that Jesus Christ is the one everlasting king of all ages. The rulers were extremely pleased to receive this letter. All people were inspired with such holy love for Antony that they wished to be called his children, for his great kindness to those who came to see him made them all devoted to him.

83. After he had refuted the pagans, advised the rulers, and comforted the brothers, Antony returned to the Inner Mountain

and to the life of discipline to which he was accustomed. There, while walking around and sitting with his visitors, he would suddenly get very quiet. After an interval of several hours, he would continue with his answer. People understood from this that he had witnessed some secret revelation. For while he was at the mountain, he saw what was happening far away and related it to others. Another time he had a very sad vision that caused him to cry profusely. While he was working with the brothers seated around him, he began to stare intently at the sky, sighing. After a time he began to shake with deep sorrow at the revelation. Immediately he knelt down before God's face and prayed that God's mercy might avert the terrible event that was about to occur. Tears followed his prayer and a great fear gripped those near him. They begged him to tell them what he had seen. Sobs racked his voice, tears tied his tongue, and groans interrupted his attempts to speak. With a loud cry of grief he managed to utter these words: "It would be better, my dear children, to die quickly to avoid the impending disaster." Tears then overcame him. In the midst of sighs of sorrow he said, "A great disaster threatens, one that no previous age has known. The catholic faith will be destroyed by a great whirlwind; men, like irrational beasts, will tear apart Christ's holy things. For I saw the altar of the Lord surrounded by a pack of donkeys that scattered everything by kicking repeatedly with their hooves. This is why I have been sighing. I heard the Lord's voice saying, 'My altar will be defiled.'" The events he warned about in this vision took place in a short time, for two years later the savage madness of the Arians erupted. Then the churches were ransacked, the divine vessels were profaned, and the pagans' foul hands defiled the sacred ministries. What wickedness. The mind recoils from repeating what happened: Virgins and married women were raped; the blood of Christ's sheep was shed in Christ's temple and spattered over the holy altars; the pagans defiled the baptistery by doing what they liked there. Antony's vision had been accurate in every detail, for the wild trampling of the mules represented the Arians' wicked behavior. But Antony comforted them in their grief by giving the following positive revelation: "My dear ones, do not give yourselves up completely to grief. For just as the Lord was angered, so he will again have pity. The church will soon regain her beauty, and you will see those who preserved the Lord's faith during the persecution shining once more with their former brightness. The serpents will return to their holes, and our religion will spread further. Just watch that the Arian filth does not stain the purity of your faith. Their teachings do not derive from the apostles but from the demons and their father, the devil."

84. Such were Antony's words. We should not find it to hard to believe that a man could perform such a great miracle. For the Savior promised this when he said: *If you have faith the size of a mustard seed, you will say to this mountain, "Move," and it will move. Nothing will be impossible for you* (Matthew 17:20). And another time the Savior said: *Very truly, I tell you, if you ask anything of the Father in my name, he will give it to you* (John 16:23). Ask and you will receive. For he himself, promising his disciples and all those who believed in him that the demons would be overcome and that many different diseases would be cured, used to say: *You received without payment, give without payment* (Matthew 10:8).

85. Was it by the authority of his own virtue that Antony healed? Did he think that what he had done was due to his own ability? His prayers, not his commands, dispelled the demons and illnesses. He accomplished all these things by calling on

the name of Christ, our God. No wise person attributes the miracle of healing to Antony, but to the Lord Jesus, who was displaying his usual benevolence to his creatures when he behaved kindly though his chosen servant. Antony merely prayed, and the Lord granted everything as a reward for Antony's virtuous life.

86. Often, though against his will, the brothers took him to the Outer Mountain. Sometimes judges arrived and asked to see Antony. But he refused, because he was annoyed by the disturbance their conversations caused. So they sent to him criminals in chains, for they knew that Antony would not be able to reject such people. Overcome by their weeping, he allowed himself to be taken to the Outer Mountain. He realized that he could help these poor people by his efforts, and he persuaded the judges who had invited him to come that they should put the fear of God before hatred and favor in giving sentence. He said that they should bear in mind the words of Scripture: *For with the judgment you make you will be judged* (Matthew 7:2). But even while he was speaking, he was thinking of his beloved solitude.

87. Forced to go there by the tears of the unfortunate prisoners, Antony gave advice that was beneficial for salvation and commended the prisoners, acquitting some of them. The commander asked him to favor them with his presence a little longer. Antony replied that he was unable to stay there further. Just as a fish taken out of water soon dies on dry land, so too, monks who stay with people from the world are soon weakened by human conversations. "For that reason," he said, "it is proper for us to hurry back to the mountain, for if we linger here we might forget our commitment to the monastic way of life." The commander marveled at the old man's great wisdom. The commander said, "Truly, this man is

God's servant. No uneducated man could possess such great wisdom unless he were guided by divine love."

88. Antony was amazingly unassuming when he advised others who came to him, urging them to forget worldly honor and to seek the happiness of a more remote life. If there were any who were oppressed by those more powerful than themselves and who were unable to obtain justice, he defended them so strenuously that he seemed to be suffering the injustice on their behalf. Many found the words he spoke useful. Many, who had abandoned great riches, were eager to join his way of life. To sum up an infinite number of points in a brief phrase, Christ granted the desert an excellent doctor. Whose sadness was not transformed in Antony's presence? Whose anger was not turned to peace? Was there anyone whose grief was not allayed by the sight of Antony? Was there anyone who did not cast off his dissatisfaction with the poverty oppressing him and immediately scorn the opulence of wealth and rejoice in his poverty? What monk who had lost his enthusiasm was not invigorated by Antony's encouragement? What young man, inflamed with desire, did not dedicate himself to chastity as a result of Antony's advice? What person, tormented by the devil, went away without a cure? Was there anyone, distracted by the enemy's thoughts, who did not have the mental disturbance clouding his perceptions dispelled and who did not go back home in a serene state of mind?

89. Antony was able to perceive each person's misfortune, for he had been granted the gift of discerning spirits on account of his virtuous life. He could therefore apply a cure for each disease, according to the wounds he found. And so it happened that as a result of his teachings all the devil's traps were exposed. There were also many girls engaged to be married. When they saw him, they turned away from marriage and

embraced mother church in their vocations. What more do I need to say? People came to him in great numbers from all over the world to see this man fighting so valiantly against the devil. No one complained that his visit to Antony had been wasted. They all found their efforts were pleasurable and delightful. They received ample compensation for the tiring nature of the journey. After his death, it was as if each person grieved for him as for his own father.

90. It is right that I should tell you about the end of his life. It teaches us some things we can all imitate. He came as usual to visit the brothers who were living at the Outer Mountain. While he was there, he learned through divine providence about his own death. He then began to speak in the following words. "My dear children, listen to your father's last thoughts. For I do not think I will see you again in this life. Nature's laws now compel me to be released from this life, after having lived for 105 years." His speech filled his listeners' hearts with sorrow, and his sad words provoked sighs and tears. They all embraced him as if he were now withdrawing from the world, but Antony spoke to them with great joy as if he were leaving foreign lands and was about to set out for his own country. He said that they should not allow idleness to creep into their way of life, and that they must guard their souls from sordid thoughts, behaving as if they were going to die each day. They should imitate the saints in all things. "And so," he said, "true faith in Christ and the religious traditions of the fathers must be protected; this is what you have learned from your reading of the Scriptures and what I have often reminded you of."

91. Antony hurriedly said goodbye to those gathered there and returned to his dwelling, the friend of his virtue. A few months later, when he began to feel some discomfort in his

aging limbs, he called two brothers who had begun to look after him in his old age. He said to them, "My dear sons, I am going the way of the fathers, to use the words of Scripture. For the Lord is now summoning me, and I long to see heaven. But I warn you who are closest to me not to waste in one moment all the hard work you have put in over a long period. You must think that it is only today that you have started on your life of religious endeavor, and you must allow the strength of your commitment to grow as if it had just begun. You are aware of the many different means the demons have of deceiving you; you have seen that their attacks are savage, but that their strength has been rendered powerless. Draw inspiration from Jesus, and set your faith in his name firmly in your minds. Then all the demons will be put to flight by the sure faith. Remember also my words of advice and the instability of the human condition. Re-examine this fluctuating life each day, and then the heavenly prize will be awarded to you without delay. Avoid, too, the poisons of the schismatics and the heretics, and seek to imitate me in hating them, because they are Christ's enemies. You yourselves know that I have never held a conciliatory conversation with them on account of their perverted will, and you know the war they persistently wage against Christ. Instead, you should be concerned to keep the Lord's commandments, so that after your death the saints may receive you into eternal tabernacles like well-known friends. Think on these things, be inspired by these things, repeat these things. And if you have any love for me, if you remember your father, let no one carry my remains to Egypt. For I do not want my body preserved. You must cover your father's humble body with earth and bury it. Also carry out this additional order given to you by this old man who is your father: Let no one other than yourselves know the place of my tomb. I trust in the Lord that this humble body will rise uncorrupt at the appointed time of the resurrection. Farewell, you who are closest to me. For Antony is departing; he will no longer be with you in this present life."

92. He had finished speaking. When his disciples had kissed him, he stretched his feet out a little and looked upon death with joy. They could tell by his cheerful expression that the holy angels who had come down to carry away his soul were present. When he saw the angels, he looked upon them as friends. Breathing out his spirit, he went to join the fathers, in accordance with the practice recorded in the Scriptures. His disciples carried out his orders. They wrapped his body as he had instructed them to do and covered it with earth. And no one apart from them knows to this day where he is buried. The legatee of the blessed Antony, who had been deemed worthy of receiving the worn cloak and the sheepskin according to Antony's orders, embraces Antony in Antony's gifts. This garment causes him to remember with joy the paragon of holiness as if a large inheritance had made him wealthy.

93. This was how Antony's life ended. These were his principal virtues. My account should help you to understand how this man of God progressed from childhood to old age, how he always trampled on any doubts, and how he never made any concessions to weariness or to his great age. Instead he kept his commitment steadfastly. He did not change his clothes or wash his feet. Nor did he request more delicate food. On account of his goodness, he retained his sharp eyesight and all his teeth, as well as his ability to walk. Contrary to the laws of nature, he kept the strength of his entire body. In fact, his body looked healthier than those glistening bodies that are pampered by baths and luxurious living.

94. To whom then, my brother, can we attribute the fact that his fame and love have spread throughout all the provinces? He became famous neither through dazzling books, nor by means of arguments of worldly wisdom, nor by means of his family's nobility, nor by the accumulation of great wealth. To whom, if not to Christ, whose gift this is? Foreseeing Antony's devotion to his divine majesty, he revealed this man who was almost hidden in another world, set in the midst of such vast areas of solitude. He revealed him all around the world. For this occurred as a result of the Creator's kindness. He always raises his servants to nobility, even against their will, so that they might learn that virtue is possible and not beyond the bonds of human nature, and so that all the best people might be compelled to imitate their lives.

Read this book carefully to the brothers so that, when they learn about the faithful life of these outstanding monks, they may know that our Savior Jesus Christ glorifies those who glorify him. He grants nobility to those who serve him and who not only long for the kingdom of heaven but also wish to lead a life of withdrawal in remote mountain places. They do this so that they themselves might win praise for their virtues and so that others may be spurred on by their examples. But if it should prove necessary, read this also to the pagans so that they may in this way recognize that our Lord Jesus Christ is God, the Son of God. They will also recognize that he grants the power to trample upon and cast out demons, which the pagans consider gods, but who really deceive and corrupt, to those who worship him diligently and who believe faithfully in him.

The Life of Paul of Thebes

by Jerome

✠

PROLOGUE

Many people have often discussed which monk was the first one to live in the desert. Some have ascribed the beginning to the blessed Elijah and to John. Of these two, Elijah seems to have been more than a monk, while John seems to have started to prophesy before he was born. Others claim that Antony was the first to live this way of life. This is partly true, for it is not so much that he came before all the others but that he inspired everyone with a commitment to this way of life. Some of Antony's disciples declare even today that a certain Paul of Thebes was the originator of the practice of the solitary life. Some people make these and other claims at their whim. They claim sometimes that there was a man living in an underground cave, with hair down to his feet, and they invent many unbelievable things that it is a waste of time to recount. Since an account of Antony has already been recorded, I have decided to write a few things about the beginning and end of Paul's life. As to how he lived during the middle years of his life and what attacks of Satan he endured, no one knows anything for sure.

✠

LIFE OF PAUL

1. During the persecutions of Christians in Rome, several
    Christians shed their blood as martyrs. At that, Christians
    yearned to be killed by the sword for Christ's name. But the
    cunning enemy wanted to murder their souls more than their
    bodies, and so he arranged for them to be killed by slow
    torture. One of the martyrs said, "Those who wished to die
    were not permitted to be killed." So that the enemy's cruelty
    might be known better, we shall include two examples to be
    sure they are not forgotten.

2. One martyr, remaining steadfast in the faith, refused to give in
    amidst the racks and the red-hot metal plates. He was covered
    with honey and placed beneath the blazing sun, with his
    hands tied behind his back, so that he might submit to mos-
    quito bites. Another young martyr was taken off to a most
    delightful garden. There, amid white lilies and red roses and
    beside a gently murmuring stream, they made him lie down
    on a thick feather bed. He was left there, tied down by soft
    garlands to prevent him escaping. When everyone had gone
    away, a beautiful prostitute came up to him and began to
    stroke his neck with gentle caresses and to touch his private
    parts with her hands. When he responded with lust, this
    shameful woman lay down on top of him. The soldier of
    Christ did not know what to do or where to turn. He had not
    yielded to tortures but he was not overcome with pleasure. At
    last, by divine inspiration, he bit off his tongue and spit it out
    in her face as she kissed him. Thus, sharp pain overcame his
    lust.

3. While these things were happening, Paul became a wealthy
    heir at the age of sixteen, after his sister's marriage and the

death of both of his parents. He was highly educated, and he was compassionate and loved God deeply. As the storm of persecution rumbled on, he withdrew to a more distant and isolated spot. But to what does the accursed greed of gold not drive the hearts of humans? His sister's husband conceived a desire to betray the person he ought to have concealed. Neither his wife's tears, nor family ties, nor God who watches everything from on high, could dissuade him from his crime. Insistently, he practiced cruelty as though it were kindness.

4. As soon as Paul realized what was happening, he fled to the mountainous regions of the desert waiting for the persecution to end, making a virtue of necessity. He would move on a bit further into the desert, then stop for a while. Repeating this pattern, he came at last to a rocky mountain, at the foot of which was a small cave. Removing the stone that blocked the cave's entrance, he began to explore more eagerly. Inside, he found a large room, open to the sky and covered by the spreading branches of a palm tree. This indicated that there was a spring of clear water, which gushed forth and was absorbed by a small crack in the ground that had produced it. There were, throughout the mountain, a number of rooms full of rusty stamps and hammers used to stamp coins. Apparently this place had been a secret factory for minting money many years ago.

5. Paul fell in love with the dwelling as if God had offered it to him. He spent the rest of his life there in prayer and solitude. The palm tree provided him with food and clothing. In case anyone should think this impossible, I call Jesus and the holy angels to witness that in some parts of the desert I have seen monks, one enclosed for thirty years, living on barley bread and muddy water. Another monk survived in an old well, living on five dried figs a day. These things will appear

incredible only to those who do not believe that everything is possible for those who believe.

6. When Paul had been living his blessed life on earth for one hundred and thirteen years, ninety-year-old Antony had been living in another part of the desert. Antony thought that no other monk in the wilderness was more perfect than he. One night while Antony was asleep God revealed to him that there was someone else in the farthest reaches of the desert who was more perfect than he and whom he ought to go and visit. As soon as the sun rose, the old man yearned to go, but he did not know where he should go. It was now noon and the sun was blazing down from the sky. But he did not turn back from his journey. He said to himself, "I believe that my God will show me my fellow servant as he has promised."

7. Antony continued on his journey, seeing nothing but wild animals' tracks and the desert's immense vastness. He did not know what to do or which way to go. Another day passed, and he could only trust that Christ would not abandon him. He spent the entire second night in prayer. In dawn's early light he saw a wolf nearby, panting thirstily and moving stealthily along the mountainside. He watched it, and when the wild beast disappeared into a cave, he went up close and tried to look inside. His curiosity was not satisfied because the darkness prevented him from seeing anything. But as Scripture says: *Perfect love casts out fear* (1 John 4:18). So, walking carefully and holding his breath, this intrepid explorer entered the cave. Going in a bit further, he stopped to listen for a sound. At last, through the terrifying darkness of the night that made it impossible to see anything, he saw a distant light. As he hurried along eagerly, he bumped his foot against a stone, making a noise. When the blessed Paul heard this noise, he closed and bolted a door that had been open.

Then Antony fell down in front of this door and begged to be allowed to come in. He said, "You know who I am, where I have come from, and why I have come. I know that I do not deserve to see you, but I will not go away unless I do. Why do you, who welcome animals, drive a person away? I have searched for you and I have found you. I knock that it may be opened to me. If I do not get what I want, I shall die here in front of your door. I trust you will bury my body when I am dead." He stood in front of the door thinking these things. Paul then said, "No one makes a request like this as a threat. No one uses tears to betray others. Are you surprised to discover I do not welcome you, since you come here with the intention of dying?" Then Paul smiled and unbolted the door. They then hugged each other, greeting each other and joining in giving thanks to the Lord.

8. After the holy kiss, Paul sat down and began to speak to Antony. "Look at the person you sought with such effort. Ugly gray hair covers his limbs, which are rotting with old age. Look upon a man who will soon be dust. But because love endures all things, tell me how humankind is getting along. Are new buildings rising up in the old cities? What government rules the world? Are there still some people alive who are in the grip of the demons' sin?" While they were talking they noticed a raven land on a tree branch. It flew down gently and placed an entire loaf of bread in front of them, much to their amazement. When it had flown away, Paul said, "Look, the Lord, who is truly loving and merciful, has sent us our supper. For the last sixty years I have always received half a loaf, but in honor of your arrival Christ has doubled his soldiers' rations."

9. When they had given the Lord thanks, they both sat down at the edge of a clear spring. Here they argued about which of

them should break the bread. They argued almost all day long. Paul argued that it was the custom for the guest to break the bread, while Antony said that the privilege belonged to the elder. Finally they decided that they should hold the bread at each end. Then if each one pulled toward himself, he would keep the bread left in his hands. Then they bent over the spring and drank a little water. Offering a sacrifice of praise to God, they passed the night in prayer. As soon as day dawned, Paul said to Antony, "It is a long time, dear brother, since I learned that you were living in these parts. It is a long time since God promised that you would be my fellow servant. But now, as the time of my death is close at hand when I will be released to be with Christ, as I have always longed to do, there remains for me a crown of righteousness now that I have run the course. You have been sent by the Lord to cover my poor body with earth, or rather, to return earth to earth."

10. When Antony heard this, he wept. He begged Paul not to leave him but to take him as his companion on that journey. But Paul said, "You ought not to seek your own benefit but that of others. It might be to your advantage to lay down the burden of the flesh and to follow the Lamb, but it is also beneficial for the other brothers to be instructed by your example. And so I beg you to go back, unless it is too much trouble, and bring me the cloak that bishop Athanasius gave you, and wrap it around my poor body." The blessed Paul asked this not because he cared particularly whether or not his corpse was clothed, but so that by going away Antony might be spared the grief caused by Paul's death. Antony was astonished that Paul knew about Athanasius and his cloak. It was as if he saw Christ in Paul, and so he worshiped God in his heart, but he did not argue with Paul. Weeping in silence,

he kissed Paul's eyes and hands and returned to the monastery. His steps could not keep up with his will. Even though his body was emaciated as a result of fasting and broken by old age, his will overcame his age.

11. He finally arrived home, breathless and exhausted. Two of his disciples, who had started looking after him in his old age, ran to him and said, "Where have you been all this time, father?" He replied, "Alas, for me, sinner that I am. It is dishonest of me to call myself a monk. I have seen Elijah. I have seen John in the desert, and now I have seen Paul in paradise." And so with his lips tightly closed, he grabbed the cloak from his prayer chamber. When his disciples begged him to explain about all this, he said, *There is a time to keep silence and a time to speak* (Ecclesiastes 3:7).

12. Then Antony went out and returned the way he had come. He failed to take even a small amount of food, for he yearned to see Paul and contemplate him with his eyes and with his whole heart. He feared the very thing that indeed had happened. He was afraid that in his absence Paul would have given up the spirit he owed to Christ. On the next morning, while he was still on his journey, he saw Paul among the hosts of angels, among the choirs of prophets and apostles, shining with a dazzling whiteness and ascending on high. Antony fell to the ground immediately and threw sand over his head. Weeping, he said, "Why do you send me away, Paul? Why are you going away without saying goodbye? Are you leaving so soon, when I have only just got to know you?"

13. The blessed Antony later reported that he had run the rest of the way with such speed that he had flown like a bird. There was good reason to hurry. For when he entered the cave he saw the lifeless corpse, in a kneeling position, its head erect and its hands stretched out to heaven. At first he thought

Paul was still alive, so he knelt down beside him to pray. But when he did not hear the praying man breathing, he fell upon him in a tearful embrace. He realized that even as a corpse the holy man, by means of his reverent posture, was praying to God, for whom all things live.

14. Antony thus wrapped Paul's body in the cloak and brought it outside, singing hymns and psalms according to the Christian tradition. But he was upset that he did not have a spade with which to dig the earth. He thought about what to do. "If I go back to the monastery, it is a four-day journey. If I stay here, I can do nothing more. Therefore let me die beside your warrior, Christ, as is fitting. Let me collapse and breathe my last breath." As he was thinking about these things, two lions came running from the inner desert. At first Antony was terrified, but when he focused his mind on God he was able to stand still without fear as if what he saw was a pair of doves. They came straight toward the corpse of the blessed old man and stopped there. Wagging their tails in devotion, they lay down at his feet, roaring loudly as if to show that they, too, were lamenting Paul's death. They then began to dig the ground near them with their paws, and they dug out a space large enough for one man. They then went straight up to Antony, their necks bent and their ears laid back. They licked his hands and feet as if demanding a reward for their hard work. He realized that they were asking him for a blessing. Immediately he burst out in praise of Christ because animals, too, understood that there is a God. He said, "O Lord, without whose assent no leaf flutters down from the tree and not a single sparrow falls to the ground, grant them what you know to be best." Making a sign to them with his hand, he ordered them to depart. As soon as they had gone away, he bent his aged shoulders beneath the burden of the

holy corpse. Laying it in the grave, he piled the earth on top of it and made a burial mound, according to custom. Before he left, he took for himself the tunic that Paul had woven out of palm leaves. He then returned to the monastery and gave the disciples a detailed account of all that had happened. He always wore Paul's tunic on Easter and Pentecost.

15. At the end of this little work, I would like to ask the wealthy, "What did this old man ever lack, naked as he was? You drink from jeweled cups, but he was satisfied with the cupped hands that nature had given him. You weave gold into your tunics, but he did not even have the shabbiest garment belonging to your slave. But then, paradise lies open to him, poor as he was, while hell will welcome you in your golden clothes. He was clothed with Christ despite his nakedness. You who are dressed in silks have lost the garment of Christ. Paul, who lies covered in the vilest dust, will rise again in glory. Heavy stone tombs press down upon you, who will burn together with your wealth. Why do you wrap your dead in cloths of gold? Why does your ostentation not cease amidst the grief and tears? Or are the corpses of the rich unable to rot except in silk clothes?"

16. I beg you, whoever you are, to remember the sinner Jerome. If the Lord would grant him his wish, he would rather choose Paul's tunic, and his rewards, than the purple robes of kings, and their punishments.

Sayings of the Fathers

✠

Antony the Great

1. When the holy father Antony lived in the desert, he was overcome with many sinful thoughts. He said to God, "Lord, I want to be saved, but these thoughts will not leave me alone. What can I do in my sickness? How can I be saved?" A short while later, when he got up to go out, Antony saw a man like himself sitting at his work, getting up from his work to pray, then sitting down to work again, and getting up again to pray. It was an angel of the Lord sent to correct and reassure him. He heard the angel saying to him: "Do this, and you will be saved." When he heard these words, Antony was filled with joy and courage. He did this, and he was saved.

2. When Antony thought about the depth of God's judgments, he asked, "Lord, how is it that some die when they are young, while others drag on to extreme old age? Why are there those who are poor and those who are rich? Why do wicked men prosper, and why are the just in need?" He heard a voice answering him, "Antony, keep your attention on yourself; these things happen according to God's judgment, and it is not to your advantage to know anything about them."

3. Someone asked Antony, "What must one do in order to please God?" He replied, "Pay attention to what I tell you. Whoever you may be, always have God before your eyes.

Whatever you do, do it according to the testimony of the holy Scriptures. Wherever you live, do not easily leave it. Keep these three precepts and you will be saved."

4. Father Antony said, "This is the great work of a person: always to take the blame for his or her own sins before God and to expect temptation until the last breath."

5. He also said, "Whoever has not experienced temptation cannot enter into the kingdom of heaven." He even added, "Without temptation no one can be saved."

6. Father Pambo asked Father Antony, "What ought I to do?" Antony replied, "Do not trust in your own righteousness, do not worry about the past, but control your tongue and your stomach."

7. Antony said, "I saw the snares that the enemy spreads out over the world, and I said, 'What can get through such snares?' Then I heard a voice saying to me, 'Humility.'"

8. He also said, "Some have afflicted their bodies by asceticism, but they lack discernment, and they are thus far from God."

9. He also said, "Our life and our death are with our neighbor. If we gain our brother, we have gained God, but if we scandalize our brother, we have sinned against God."

10. Antony said, "Just as fish die if they stay too long out of water, so the monks who loiter outside their prayer chambers or pass their time with men of the world lose the intensity of their inner peace. So, like a fish going toward the sea, we must hurry to reach our prayer chamber. If we delay outside, we will lose our interior watchfulness."

11. He said, "One who wishes to live in solitude in the desert is delivered from three conflicts: hearing, speech, and sight. There is only one conflict for him, and that is sexual temptations."

12. Some brothers came to find Father Antony to tell him about the visions they were having, and to find out from him if the

visions were true or if they came from demons. They had a donkey that died along the way. When they reached the place where the old man was, he said to them, before they could ask him anything, "How was it that the little donkey died on the way here?" They said, "How do you know about that, Father?" And he told them, "The demons showed me what happened." So they said, "That was what we came to ask you about. We were afraid we were being deceived, for we have visions that often turn out to be true." Thus the old man convinced them, using the example of the donkey, that their visions came from the demons.

13. A hunter in the desert saw Antony enjoying himself with the brothers, and he was shocked. Wanting to show him that it was necessary sometimes to meet the needs of the brothers, the old man said to him, "Put an arrow in your bow and shoot it." So he did. The old man then said, "Shoot another," and the hunter said, "If I bend my bow so much I will break it." Then the old man said to him, "It is the same with God's work. If we stretch the brothers beyond measure they will soon break. Sometimes it is necessary to come down to meet their needs." When he heard these words, the hunter regretted he had said anything, and he went away greatly edified by the old man. The brothers went home stronger.

14. Antony heard of a young monk who had performed a miracle on the road. Seeing the old men walking with difficulty along the road, he ordered the wild donkeys to come and carry them until they reached Antony. Those whom they had carried told this story to Antony. He said to them, "This monk seems to be a ship loaded with goods but I do not know if he will reach harbor." After a while, Antony suddenly began to weep, to tear his hair and lament. His disciples said to him, "Why are you weeping, Father?" The old man replied, "A

great pillar of the church has just fallen (he was referring to the young monk); but go to him, and see what has happened." So the disciples went and found the monk sitting on a mat and weeping for the sin he had committed. Seeing the disciples of the old man he said, "Tell the old man to pray that God will give me just ten days, and I hope I will have made satisfaction." But in the space of five days he died.

15. The brothers praised a monk before Antony. When the monk came to see him, Antony wanted to know how he would bear insults. Seeing that he could not bear them at all, Antony said to him, "You are like a village magnificently decorated on the outside, but destroyed from within by robbers."

16. Someone said to Antony, "Pray for me." The old man said to him, "I will have no mercy upon you, nor will God have any, if you yourself do not make an effort, and if you do not pray to God."

17. One day some old men came to see Antony. Father Joseph was in their midst. Wanting to test them, the old man suggested a text from the Scriptures, and, beginning with the youngest, he asked them what it meant. Each gave his opinion, as he was able. But to each one the old man said, "You have not understood it." Finally he said to Joseph, "How would you explain this saying?" Joseph said, "I do not know." Then Antony said, "Indeed, Joseph has found the way, for he has said, 'I do not know.'"

18. Some brothers were coming from another town to see Antony. As they were getting into a boat to go there, they found an old man who also wanted to go there. The brothers did not know him. They sat in the boat, occupied by turns with the words of the Fathers, the Scriptures, and their manual work. But the old man remained silent. When they arrived on the shore, they found that the old man was going

to Antony's prayer chamber, too. When they reached the place, Antony said to them, "You found this old man a good companion for the journey?" Then he said to the old man, "You have brought many good brothers with you, Father." The old man said, "No doubt they are good, but they talk in an unguarded fashion and say whatever comes into their mouths."

19. The brothers came to Antony and said to him, "Tell us: How are we to be saved?" The old man said to them, "You have heard the Scriptures. That should teach you how." But they said, "We want to hear from you, too, Father." Then the old man said to them, "The Gospel says: *If anyone strikes you on the right cheek, turn the other also*" (Matthew 5:39). They said, "We cannot do that." The old man said, "If you cannot offer the other cheek, at least allow one cheek to be struck." "We cannot do that, either," they said. So he said, "If you are not able to do that, do not return evil for evil," and they said, "We cannot do that, either." Then the old man said to his disciple, "Prepare a little brew of corn for these invalids. If you cannot do this, or that, what can I do for you? What you need is prayers."

20. Someone renounced the world and gave his goods to the poor, but he kept back a little for his personal expenses. He went to see Antony. When he told him this, the old man said to him, "If you want to be a monk, go into the village, buy some meat, cover your naked body with it and come here like that." The brother did so, and the dogs and birds tore at his flesh. When he came back, the old man asked him whether or not he had followed his advice. He showed him his wounded body, and Antony said, "Those who renounce the world but want to keep something for themselves are torn this way by demons that make war on them."

21. One day a monk in another monastery was tempted. Cast out of the monastery, he went over the mountain to Antony. The

brother lived near him for a while, and then Antony sent him back to the monastery from which he had been expelled. When the brothers saw him, they cast him out again. He returned to Antony, saying, "My Father, they will not receive me." Then the old man sent them a message saying, "A boat was shipwrecked at sea and lost its cargo. It reached the shore with great difficulty. You want to throw into the sea that which has found a safe harbor on the shore." When the brothers understood that it was Antony who had sent them this monk, they received him at once.

22. Antony said, "I believe that the body possesses a natural movement, to which it is adapted, but which it cannot follow without the consent of the soul. It only signifies in the body a movement without passion. There is another movement, which comes from the nourishment and warming of the body by eating and drinking. This causes the heat of the blood to stir up the body to work. That is why Paul said: *Do not get drunk with wine, for that is debauchery* (Ephesians 5:18). And in the Gospel, the Lord also recommends this to his disciples: *Be on guard so that your hearts are not weighed down with dissipation and drunkenness* (Luke 21:34). But there is yet another movement that afflicts those who fight, and that comes from the wiles and jealousy of the demons. You must understand what these three bodily movements are: One is natural, one comes from eating too much food, the third is caused by the demons."

23. He also said, "God does not allow the same warfare and temptations to this generation as he did to earlier generations. For people are weaker now and cannot bear so much."

24. Antony had a revelation in his desert that there was one who was his equal in the city. He was a doctor by profession, and whatever he had beyond his needs he gave to the poor. Every day he sang the Sanctus with the angels.

25. Antony said, "A time is coming when men will go mad, and when they see someone who is not mad, they will attack him, saying, 'You are mad; you are not like us.'"

26. The brothers asked Antony to interpret a passage from the book of Leviticus. The old man went out into the desert. Father Ammonas secretly followed Antony into the desert. Antony went far into the desert and prayed, crying out in a loud voice, "God, send Moses to make me understand this saying." Then a voice came to Antony. Father Ammonas said that he heard a voice speaking to Antony, but he could not understand what it said.

27. Three fathers used to go and visit Antony every year. Two of them used to discuss their thoughts and the salvation of their souls with him, but the third always remained silent and did ask any questions. After a long time, Antony said to him, "You often come here to see me, but you never ask me anything." The other replied, "It is enough for me to see you, Father."

28. They said that a certain old man asked God to let him see the fathers, and he saw them all except Antony. So he asked his guide, "Where is Antony?" He told him that wherever the old man found God, he would find Antony there.

29. Someone in a monastery was falsely accused of sexual sins, and he arose and went to see Antony. The brothers also came from the monastery to correct him and take him back. They tried to prove that he had done this thing, but he defended himself and denied that he had done anything of the kind. Now Cephalus happened to be there and he told this parable: "I have seen a man on the bank of the river buried up to his knees in mud, and some men came to give him a hand to help him out. But they pushed him further in up to his neck." Then Antony said this about Cephalus: "Here is a real man, who can care for souls and save them." Everyone there was

pierced to the heart by Antony's words, and they asked the brother's forgiveness. So, scolded by the fathers, they took the brother back to the monastery.

30. Some say that the Holy Spirit carried Antony along, but he would never talk about this with men. Such men see what is happening in the world, as well as knowing what is going to happen.

31. One day Antony received a letter from Constantine asking him to come to Constantinople. He wondered whether he ought to go, and he asked his disciple his thoughts. The follower said, "If you go, you will be called simply Antony, but if you stay here you will be called Father Antony."

32. Antony said, "I no longer fear God, but I love him. For love casts out fear."

33. He also said, "Always have the fear of God before your eyes. Remember him who gives death and life. Hate the world and all that is in it. Hate all peace that comes from the flesh. Renounce this life, so that you may be alive to God. Remember what you have promised God, for it will be required of you on the day of judgment. Suffer hunger, thirst, nakedness; be watchful and sorrowful; weep, and groan in your heart; test yourselves, to see if you are worthy of God; despise the flesh, so that you may preserve your souls."

34. Antony once went to visit Father Amoun. Father Amoun said, "By your prayers, the number of brothers increases, and some of them want to build more prayer chambers where they may live in peace. How far away from here do you think we should build the prayer chambers?" Antony said, "Let us eat at the ninth hour and then let us go for a walk in the desert and explore the country." So they went out into the desert and they walked until sunset. Then Antony said, "Let us pray and plant the cross here, so that those who wish to do so may

build here. Then when those who remain there want to visit those who have come here, they can take a little food at the ninth hour and then come. If they do this, they will be able to keep in touch with each other without distraction of mind."

35. Antony said, "Whoever hammers a lump of iron, first decides what he is going to make from it. Even so we ought to make up our minds what kind of virtue we want to forge, or we labor in vain."

36. He also said, "Obedience with abstinence gives men power over wild beasts."

37. He also said, "Nine monks fell away after many labors and were obsessed with spiritual pride. They put their trust in their own works. So deceived, they did not heed properly the commandment that says, 'Ask your father and he will tell you.'"

38. And he said this, "If he is able to, a monk ought to tell his elders confidently how many steps he takes and how many drops of water he drinks in his prayer chamber, in case he is in error about it."

✠

BASIL THE GREAT

1. One of the old men said, "When Saint Basil came to the monastery one day, he said to the abbot, 'Do you have someone here who is obedient?' The other replied, 'They are all your servants, master, and strive for their salvation.' But he repeated, 'Do you have someone who is really obedient?' Then the abbot led a brother to him, and Saint Basil used him to serve during the meal. When the meal ended, the brother

brought him some water for rinsing his hands. Saint Basil said to him, 'Come here, so I may also offer water to you.' The brother allowed the bishop to pour the water. Then Saint Basil said to him, 'When I enter the sanctuary, come, so that I may ordain you deacon.' When this was done, he ordained him priest and took him with him to the bishop's palace because of his obedience."

✠

GREGORY THE THEOLOGIAN

1. Father Gregory said, "These three things God requires of all the baptized: right faith in the heart, truth on the tongue, and temperance in the body."
2. He also said. "The entire life of humankind is but one single day for those who are working hard with longing."

✠

GERONTIUS

1. Father Gerontius said that many, tempted by the pleasures of the body, commit sexual sins, not in their body only but also in their spirit. Thus, while preserving their body's purity, they commit prostitution in their soul. "Thus it is good, my well-beloved, to do that which is written, and for each one to guard his own heart with all possible care."

✠

EPHREM

1. While yet a child, Ephrem had a dream and then a vision. A branch of vine came out of his tongue, grew bigger, and filled everything under heaven. It was full of beautiful fruit. All the birds of heaven came to eat of the fruit of the vine, and the more they ate, the more the fruit increased.

2. Another time, one of the saints had a vision. According to the commandment of God, a band of angels descended from heaven, holding in their hands a piece of papyrus covered with writing. They said to one another, "To whom should we give this?" Some said, "To this one," others, "To that one." Then the answer came in these words, "Truly, they are holy and righteous, but none of them is able to receive this except Ephrem." The old man saw that the papyrus was given to Ephrem, and he saw a fountain flowing from his lips. Then he understood that the Holy Spirit came out of Ephrem's lips.

3. Another time, when Ephrem was on the road, a prostitute tried to flatter Ephrem into having sex with her, or at least to make him angry with her; for no one had ever seen him angry. He said to her, "Follow me." When they had reached a very crowded place, he said to her, "Let's do whatever you desire in this place." But, seeing the crowd, she said to him, "How can we do what we want to do in front of so great a crowd, without being ashamed?" He said, "If you blush before men, how much more should we blush before God, who knows what is hidden in darkness?" She was covered with shame and went away without having achieved anything.

✠

AMOUN OF NITRIA

1. Father Amoun once came to see Father Antony and said to him, "Since my rule is stricter than yours, how is it that your name is better known than mine is?" Antony answered, "It is because I love God more than you."

2. Amoun went to find Father Poemen and said to him, "When I go to my neighbor's room, or when he comes to mine for some need or other, we are afraid of talking to each other, for we are afraid we might start talking about some worldly subjects." The old man replied, "You are right, for young men need to be careful to watch themselves." Then Amoun continued, "But what do the old men do?" He replied, "The old men who have advanced in virtue have nothing in them that is worldly; there is nothing worldly in their mouths of which they could speak." "But," Amoun replied, "When I am obliged to speak to my neighbor, do you prefer that I speak of the Scriptures or of the sayings of the Fathers?" The old man answered him, "If you can't be silent, you had better talk about the sayings of the Fathers rather than about the Scriptures. It is not so dangerous."

✠

ANOUB

1. Father Anoub said, "Since the day I took on the calling of Christ, I have not lied."

✠

ABRAHAM

1. There was once a story about an old man who for fifty years
   had neither eaten bread nor drunk wine readily. He even said,
   "I have destroyed my yearnings for lust, avarice, and pride."
   Learning what the man had said, Father Abraham came and
   said to him, "Did you really say that?" "Yes," said the man.
   Then Abraham said to him, "If you were to find a woman
   lying on your mat when you entered your room, would you
   think that it is not a woman?" "No," he replied, "but I would
   struggle with my thoughts so as not to touch her." Then
   Father Abraham said, "Then you have not destroyed the
   passion, but it still lives in you, although it is controlled.
   Again, if you are walking and you see some gold among the
   stones and shells, can your spirit regard them all as of equal
   value?" "No," he replied, "but I would struggle with my
   thoughts so as not to take the gold." The old man said to him,
   "See, greed still lives in you, though it is controlled."
   Abraham continued, "Suppose you learn that one of two
   brothers loves you and the other hates you and speaks evil of
   you. If they come to see you, will you receive both of them
   with the same love?" "No," the other replied, "but I would
   struggle with my thoughts so I could be as kind to the one
   who hates me as I am to the one who loves me." Abraham
   said to him, "So, then, the passions continue to live; it is
   simply that you have learned with God's help to control
   them."

✠

APOLLO

1. There was in the monasteries an old man called Apollo. If someone came to see him about doing a piece of work, he would set out joyfully, saying, "I am going to work with Christ today, for the salvation of my soul, for that is the reward he gives."

2. When he taught about how to welcome others, Apollo said that one should bow before the brothers who come. We should do this since it is God, not the brothers themselves, before whom we are bowing. "When you see your brother," he said, "you see the Lord your God." He added, "We have learned that from Abraham (cf. Genesis 18). When you receive the brothers, invite them to rest awhile, for this is what we learn from Lot, who invited the angels to do so" (cf. Genesis 19:3).

✠

ANDREW

1. Father Andrew said, "These three things are appropriate for a monk: exile, poverty, and endurance in silence."

✠

DIOSCORUS

1. People said that Father Dioscorus ate bread made of barley and lentils. Every year he made a resolution about a particular

thing, saying, "I will not meet anyone this year"; or else, "I will not speak"; or else, "I will not eat cooked food"; or else, "I will not eat fruit or vegetables." He acted this way in all his work. When he accomplished one thing, he began another. He did this every year.

2. Someone once questioned Father Poemen: "My thoughts often disturb me, making me put my sins aside. My thoughts are then occupied with my brother's faults." The old man told him the following story about Father Dioscorus: "In his room he wept over himself, while his disciple was sitting in another prayer chamber. When the latter came to see the old man he asked him, 'Father, why are you weeping?' 'I am weeping over my sins,' the old man answered him. Then his disciple said, 'You do not have any sins, Father.' The old man replied, 'Truly, my child, if I were allowed to see my sins, three or four people would not be enough to weep for them.'"

✠

DOULAS

1. Father Doulas said, "If the enemy persuades us to give up our inner peace, we must not listen to him. For nothing is equal to this peace and the lack of food. These two join together to fight the enemy. They make interior vision keen."

2. He also said, "Detach yourself from the love of the multitude unless you want your enemy to question your spirit and trouble your inner peace."

✠

EPIPHANIUS, BISHOP OF CYPRUS

1. One day Saint Epiphanius sent someone to Father Hilarion with this request: "Come, and let us see one another before we depart from the body." When he came, they rejoiced in each other's company. During their meal, they were brought a fowl; Epiphanius took it and gave it to Hilarion. Then the old man said to him, "Forgive me, but since I received the habit I have not eaten meat that has been killed." Then Epiphanius answered, "Since I took the habit, I have not allowed anyone to go to sleep with a complaint against me, and I have not gone to rest with a complaint against anyone." The old man replied, "Forgive me, your way of life is better than mine."

2. The same old man said, "The Canaanite woman cries out, and she is heard (Matthew 15); the woman with the issue of blood is silent, and she is called blessed (Luke 8); the Pharisee speaks, and he is condemned (Matthew 9); the publican does not open his mouth, and he is heard (Luke 18)."

3. He also said, "The acquisition of Christian books is necessary for those who can use them. For the mere sight of these books renders us less inclined to sin, and encourages us to believe more firmly in righteousness."

4. He also said, "Reading the Scriptures is a great safeguard against sin."

5. Epiphanius said, "It is a great treachery to know nothing of the divine law."

6. He also said, "Ignorance of the Scriptures is at once a steep and dangerous cliff and a deep abyss."

7. Epiphanius said, "The righteous sin through their mouths, but the unrighteous sin in their whole bodies. This is why David

sings: *Set a watch, O LORD, before my mouth; keep the door of my lips* (Psalm 141:3 KJV). And he also says: *I will take heed to my ways, that I sin not with my tongue*" (Psalm 39:1 KJV).

✠

EVAGRIUS

1. Father Evagrius said, "Sit in your prayer chamber, collecting your thoughts. Remember the day of your death. See then what the death of your body will be; let your spirit be heavy, take pains, condemn the vanity of the world, so as to be able to live always in the peace you have in view without weakening. Remember also what happens in hell, and think about the state of the souls down there, their painful silence, their most bitter groanings, their fear, their strife, their waiting. Think of their grief without end and the tears their souls shed eternally. But keep the day of resurrection and of presentation to God in remembrance also. Imagine the fearful and terrible judgment. Consider the fate kept for sinners, their shame before the face of God and the angels and archangels and all men, that is to say, the punishments, the eternal fire, the worms that do not rest, the darkness, the gnashing of teeth, the fear, and the supplications. Consider also the good things in store for the righteous: confidence in the face of God the Father and his Son, the angels and archangels and all the people of the saints, the kingdom of heaven, and the gifts of that realm, joy and beatitude. Remember well these two realities. Weep for the judgment of sinners; afflict yourself for fear lest you too feel those pains. But rejoice and be glad at the lot of the righteous. Strive to obtain those joys, but be a stranger to those pains. Whether you are inside or outside

your prayer chamber, be careful that you never forget these things, so that you may at least flee wrong and harmful thoughts."

2. He also said, "Restrain yourself from affection toward many people, out of fear that your spirit may be distracted, and so that your interior peace may not be disturbed."

3. He also said, "It is a great thing to pray without distraction, but to chant psalms without distraction is even greater."

4. He also said, "Always keep your death in mind, and do not forget the eternal judgment; then there will be no fault in your soul."

5. He also said, "Take away temptations, and no one will be saved."

✠

THEODORA

Theodora was one of the great women ascetics of the desert. Palladius mentions Theodora, "the wife of the tribune, who reached such a depth of poverty that she became a recipient of alms and finally died in the monastery of Hesychas near the sea." She consulted Archbishop Theophilus and appears to have been consulted by many monks about the monastic life.

1. Mother Theodora asked Archbishop Theophilus about some words of the Apostle, saying, "What does this mean, *making the most of the time?*" (Colossians 4:5). He said to her, "This saying shows us how to profit at all times. For example, is it a time of excess for you? Through humility and patience buy up the time of excess, and draw profit from it. Is it a time of shame? Buy it up by means of resignation and win it. So

everything that goes against us can, if we wish, become profitable to us."

2.   Mother Theodora said, "Let us strive to enter by the narrow gate. Just as the trees, if they have not stood before the winter's storms, cannot bear fruit, so it is with us. This present age is a storm, and it is only through many trials and temptations that we can obtain an inheritance in the kingdom of heaven."

3.   She also said, "It is good to live in peace, for the wise person practices perpetual prayer. It is truly a great thing for a virgin or a monk to live in peace, especially for the younger ones. However, you should realize that as soon as you intend to live in peace, evil at once comes and weighs down your soul through faintheartedness and evil thoughts. It also attacks your body through sickness, debility, weakening of the knees, and all the members. It dissipates the strength of soul and body, so that one believes one is ill and no longer able to pray. But if we are watchful, all these temptations fall away. There was, in fact, a monk who was seized by cold and fever every time he began to pray, and he suffered from headaches, too. In this condition, he said to himself, 'I am ill, and near to death, so now I will get up before I die and pray.' By reasoning this way, he did violence to himself and prayed. When he had finished, the fever abated also. So, by reasoning in this way, the brother resisted and prayed, and was able to conquer his thoughts."

4.   The same Mother Theodora said, "A devout man happened to be insulted by someone, and he said to the person, 'I could say as much to you, but God's commandment keeps my mouth shut.'"

5.   The same Mother said that a teacher ought to be a stranger to the desire for domination, vanity, and pride. One should not be able to fool him by flattery, nor blind him by gifts, nor

conquer him by the stomach, nor dominate him by anger. But he should be patient, gentle, and humble as far as possible. He must be tested and, without showing favoritism, full of concern, and a lover of souls.

6. She also said that neither asceticism, nor vigils, nor any kind of suffering is able to save. Only true humility can do that. She said that there once was a desert monk who was able to banish the demons; and he asked them, "What makes you go away? Is it fasting?" They replied, "We do not eat or drink." "Is it vigils?" They replied, "We do not sleep." "Is it separation from the world?" "We live in the deserts." "What power sends you away, then?" They said, "Nothing can overcome us, but only humility." Then she said, "Do you see how humility is victorious over the demons?"

7. The same Mother was asked about the conversations one hears: "If one is habitually listening to secular speech, how can one yet live for God alone, as you suggest?" She said, "Just as when you are sitting at table and there are many courses, you take some but without pleasure. So when secular conversations come your way, have your heart turned toward God. Thanks to this disposition, you will hear them without pleasure, and they will not do you any harm."

8. Another of the old men questioned Mother Theodora saying, "At the resurrection of the dead, how shall we rise?" She said, "We have Christ our God, the one who died and rose again for us, as our example and prototype."

✠

JOHN THE DWARF

1. People said that Father John the Dwarf withdrew and lived in the desert with an old man of Thebes. His spiritual guide took a piece of dry wood, planted it, and said to him, "Water it every day with a bottle of water, until it bears fruit." Now the water was so far away that he had to leave in the evening and return the following morning. At the end of three years the wood came to life and bore fruit. Then the old man took some of the fruit and carried it to the church, saying to the brothers, "Take and eat the fruit of obedience."

3. Father John the Dwarf said, "If a king wanted to take possession of his enemy's city, he would begin by cutting off the water and the food, so his enemies, dying of hunger, would submit to him. It is the same with the passions of the flesh: If a person goes about fasting and hungry, the enemies of his soul grow weak."

4. Some old men were entertaining themselves by having a meal together. Father John was among them. A venerable priest got up to offer drink, but nobody accepted any from him, except John the Dwarf. They were surprised and said to him, "How is it that you, the youngest, dared to let yourself be served by the priest?" Then he said to them, "When I get up to offer drink, I am glad when everyone accepts it, since I am receiving my reward. That is the reason, then, that I accepted it, so that he also might gain his reward and not be grieved by seeing that no one would accept anything from him." When they heard this, they were all filled with wonder and edification at his discretion.

5. The brothers used to tell how they were sitting one day at a love feast and one brother at table began to laugh. When he

saw that, Father John began to weep, saying, "What does this brother have in his heart, that he should laugh, when he ought to weep, because he is eating at a love feast?"

6. Some people came one day to test Father John to see whether he would let himself be distracted and speak of the things of this world. They said to him, "We give thanks to God that this year there has been much rain and the palm trees have been able to drink, and their shoots have grown, and the brothers have found manual work." Father John said to them, "So it is when the Holy Spirit descends into the hearts of men; they are renewed and they put forth leaves in the fear of God."

7. Father John said, "I am like a man sitting under a great tree, who sees wild beasts and snakes coming against him in great numbers. When he cannot withstand them any longer, he runs to climb the tree and is saved. It is just the same with me. I sit in my prayer chamber and I am aware of evil thoughts coming against me. When I have no more strength against them, I take refuge in God by prayer and I am saved from the enemy."

8. Father Poemen said of Father John the Dwarf that he had prayed that God would take his passions away from him so that he might become free from care. He went and told an old man this: "I find myself in peace, without an enemy." The old man said to him, "Go, ask God to stir up warfare so that you may regain the affliction and humility that you used to have. For it is by warfare that the soul makes progress." So he sought God, and when warfare came, he no longer prayed that it might be taken away, but said, "Lord, give me strength for the fight."

9. The old man also said this to someone about the soul that wishes to be converted: "There was in a city a courtesan who

had many lovers. One of the governors approached her, saying, 'Promise me you will be good, and I will marry you.' She promised this and he took her and brought her to his house. Her lovers, seeking her again, said to one another, 'That lord has taken her with him to his house. If we go to his house and he learns of it, he will condemn us. But let us go to the back, and whistle to her. Then, when she recognizes the sound of the whistle, she will come down to us. As for us, we shall be unassailable.' When she heard the whistle, the woman stopped her ears and withdrew to the inner chamber and shut the doors." The old man said that this courtesan is our soul, that her lovers are the passions and other men; that the lord is Christ; that the inner chamber is the eternal dwelling; those who whistle are the evil demons, but the soul always takes refuge in the Lord.

10. Father John said, "Who sold Joseph?" A brother replied, "His brothers." The old man said to him, "No, it was his humility that sold him, because he could have said, 'I am your brother' and have objected. But, because he kept silence, he sold himself by his humility. It is also his humility that set him up chief in Egypt."

12. He also said, "Humility and the fear of God are above all virtues."

13. The same Father said to his disciple, "Let us honor one only, and everyone will honor us; for if we despise one, that is God, everyone will despise us, and we will be lost."

14. People said that Father John went to church one day and he heard some brothers arguing. So he returned to his prayer chamber. He went round it three times and then went in. Some people who had seen him, wondered why he had done this. They went and asked him. He said to them, "My ears were full of that argument, so I circled round in order to purify

them, and thus I entered my prayer chamber with my mind at rest."

15. Father John said, "I think it best that a man should have a little bit of all the virtues. Therefore, get up early every day and acquire the beginning of every virtue and every commandment of God. Use great patience in the love of God, with all the fervor of your soul and body. Exercise great humility; bear with interior distress; be watchful and pray often with reverence, with purity of speech and control of your eyes. When people despise you, do not get angry; be at peace, and do not render evil for evil. Do not pay attention to the faults of others, and do not try to compare yourself with others, knowing you are less than every created thing. Renounce everything material and that which is of the flesh. Live by the cross, in warfare, in poverty of spirit, in voluntary spiritual asceticism, in fasting, penitence, and tears, in discernment, in purity of soul, taking hold of that which is good. Do your work in peace. Persevere in keeping vigil, in hunger and thirst, in cold and nakedness, and in sufferings. Shut yourself in a tomb as though you were already dead, so that at all times you will think death is near."

16. Father John the Dwarf said, "A house is not built by beginning at the top and working down. You must begin with the foundations in order to reach the top." They said to him, "What does this saying mean?" He said, "The foundation is our neighbor, whom we must win, and that is the place to begin. For all the commandments of Christ depend on this one."

17. Father John said to his brother, "Even if we are entirely despised in people's eyes, we should rejoice that we are honored in God's eyes."

18. Father John said that the saints are like a group of trees, each bearing different fruits but watered from the same source. The practices of one saint differ from those of another, but it is the same Spirit that works in all of them.

19. Father John also said: "You know the first blow the devil gave to Job was through his possessions. He saw that Job had not grieved or separated himself from God. With the second blow, he touched his flesh, but the brave man did not sin by any words from his mouth. In fact, he had within his heart that which is of God, and he drew on this source unceasingly."

✠

ISIDORE THE PRIEST

1. Isidore said that for forty years he had been tempted to sin in thought, but that he had never given in either to greed or to anger.

2. He also said, "When I was younger and remained in my monastery room, I set no limit to prayer; the night was for me as much the time of prayer as the day."

3. Father Isidore went one day to see Father Theophilus, the archbishop in the city of Alexandria. When Isidore returned, people asked him, "What is going on in the city?" But he said to them, "Truly, brothers, I did not see the face of anyone there, except that of the archbishop." Hearing this, they were very anxious and said to him, "Has there been a disaster there, then, Father?" He said, "Not at all. But the thought of looking at anyone did not get the better of me." When they heard these words they were filled with admiration, and were strengthened in their intention of guarding the eyes from all distraction.

4. The same Father Isidore said, "It is the wisdom of the saints to recognize the will of God. Indeed, in obeying the truth, people surpass everything else, for they are the image and likeness of God. Of all evil suggestions, the most terrible is that of following one's own heart, that is to say, one's own thought, and not the law of God. A person who does this will be afflicted later on because he has not recognized the mystery, and he has not found the way of the saints in order to work in it. For now is the time to labor for the Lord. For salvation is found in the day of affliction. For it is written: *By your endurance you will gain your souls*" (Luke 21:19).

5. Father Poemen also said that wherever Father Isidore addressed people in church he said only one thing, "Forgive your brother, so that you also may be forgiven."

✠

ISIDORE OF PELUSIA

1. Father Isidore of Pelusia said, "To live without speaking is better than to speak without living. For the former, who lives rightly, does good even by his silence; but the latter does no good even when he speaks. When words and life correspond to one another they are together the whole of philosophy."

2. The same Father said, "Prize the virtues, and do not be the slave of glory for, the former are immortal, while the latter soon fades."

3. He also said, "Many desire virtue, but fear to go forward in the way that leads to it, while others consider that virtue does not even exist. So it is necessary to persuade the former to give up their habitual idleness, and to teach the others what virtue really is."

4. He also said, "Vice takes men away from God and separates them from one another. So we must turn from it quickly and pursue virtue, which leads to God and unites us with another. Now, the definition of virtue and of philosophy is this: simplicity with prudence."

5. He also said, "The heights of humility are great, and so are the depths of boasting; I advise you to attend to the first and not to fall into the second."

6. He also said, "The desire for possessions is dangerous and terrible, knowing no satiety; it drives the soul that it controls to the heights of evil. Therefore, let us drive it away vigorously from the beginning. For once it has become master, it cannot be overcome."

✠

CASSIAN

1. Father Cassian said, "There was an old man who was served by a holy virgin, and people said he was not pure. The old man heard what they said about him. Near his death, he said to the fathers, 'When I am dead, plant my stick in the grave; if it grows and bears fruit, know that I am pure from all contact with her, but if it does not grow, know that I have sinned with her.' So they planted the stick, and on the third day it budded and bore fruit, and they all gave glory to God."

2. Cassian once told this story: "Father John, abbot of a great monastery, went to see another father who had been living for forty years very far off in the desert. As he was very fond of him and could therefore speak freely with him, he said to him, 'What good have you done by living here in retreat for so long, and not being easily disturbed by anyone?' He

replied, 'Since I lived in solitude the sun has never seen me eating.' Father John said to him, 'As for me, it has never seen me angry.'"

✠

MACARIUS THE GREAT

1. Father Macarius said, "If slander has become to you the same as praise, poverty as riches, deprivation as abundance, you will not die. Indeed, it is impossible for anyone who firmly believes, who labors with devotion, to fall into the impurity of the passions and be led astray by the demons."

2. Father Paphnutius, a disciple of Father Macarius, said, "I asked my Father to say a word to me." He replied, "Do no evil to anyone, and do not judge anyone. Observe this and you will be saved."

3. Father Macarius said, "Do not associate with those who have bad reputations."

4. Father Macarius said, "If we keep remembering the wrongs that people have done us, we destroy the power of the remembrance of God. But if we remind ourselves of the evil deeds of the demons, we shall be invulnerable."

5. Someone said to Macarius, "Please tell me something of value." Macarius said to him, "Flee from people, stay in your prayer room, cry over your sins, do not take pleasure in the conversation of people, and you will be saved."

✠

ARSENIUS

1. Someone questioned Father Arsenius, desiring to hear a word from him, and the old man said to him, "Strive with all your might to bring your interior activity into accord with God, and you will overcome exterior passions."

2. He also said, "If we seek God, he will show himself to us, and if we keep him, he will remain close to us."

✠

AGATHON

1. Father Peter once told this story of Father Agathon: "One day when I was in Father Agathon's prayer chamber, a brother came in and said to him, 'I want to live with the brothers; tell me how I can do so.' The old man answered, 'As long as you live, continue to think of yourself as the stranger you were on the first day you joined them, so as not to become too familiar with them.' Father Macarius asked, 'And what does this familiarity produce?' The old man replied, "It is like a strong, burning wind, sweeping everything away, and destroying the fruit of the trees." So Father Macarius said, "Is speaking too freely really all that bad?" Agathon said, "No passion is worse than an uncontrolled tongue, because it is the mother of all the passions. Accordingly, the good workman should not use it, even if he is living alone in his prayer chamber. I know a brother who spent a long time in his prayer chamber using a small bed, who said, 'If no one had told me about the bed in my prayer chamber, I would have left my prayer chamber without using it.' The hard-working monk is a warrior."

2. Agathon said, "The monk should not let his conscience accuse him of anything."

3. He also said, "A person cannot make progress, not even in a single virtue, unless he keeps the commandments of God."

4. He also said, "I have never held too deep a grievance against anyone, and, as far as I could, I have never let anyone hold too deep a grievance against me."

5. Having heard about Agathon's great discernment, some monks came to find him. Wanting to see if he would lose his temper, they said to him "Aren't you that Agathon who people say is an adulterer and a proud man?" "Yes, it is very true," he answered. They resumed, "Aren't you that Agathon who is always talking nonsense?" "I am." Again they said, "Aren't you Agathon the heretic? At this he replied, "I am not a heretic." So they asked him, "Tell us why you accepted everything we said to you, but repudiated this last insult." He replied, "The first accusations I take to heart, for that is good for my soul. But heresy is separation from God. I have no wish to be separated from God." At this saying they were astonished at his discernment and returned, edified.

6. People said that Father Agathon spent a long time building a retreat with his disciples. When it was finished, they came to live there. Seeing something during the first week that seemed to him harmful, he said to his disciples, "Get up, let us leave this place." But they were dismayed and replied, "If you had already decided to move, why have we taken so much trouble building this place? We will be humiliated, for people will say, 'Look at them, moving again; what unstable people!'" He saw that their reticence held them back, so he said to them, "Even if some people say those things, others will be guided spiritually and say, 'How blessed are they who go away for God's sake, having no other care.' However, let

those who want to come, come; as for me, I am going." Then they bowed on the ground before him and asked him to allow them to go with him.

7. People said that Father Agathon often went away, taking nothing but his knife for making wicker-baskets.

8. Someone asked Father Agathon, "Which is better, bodily asceticism or interior watchfulness?" The old man replied, "Humankind is like a tree; bodily asceticism is the leaves, interior watchfulness the fruit. As the Scriptures say, *Every tree therefore that does not bear good fruit is cut down and thrown into the fire* (Matthew 3:10). All our care should be directed toward the fruit, but it needs the protection and the adornment of the leaves, which is bodily asceticism."

9. The brothers also asked him, "Which virtue requires the greatest effort among all the good works?" He answered, "Forgive me, but I think there is no labor greater than prayer to God. For every time a man wants to pray, his enemies, the demons, want to prevent him. For they know that it is only by turning him from prayer that they can hinder his journey. Whatever good work a man undertakes, if he perseveres in it, he will attain rest. But prayer is warfare to the last breath."

10. Father Agathon was wise in spirit and active in body. He provided everything he needed for himself, in manual work, food, and clothing.

11. Father Agathon was walking with his disciples. One of them, finding a small green pea on the road, said to the old man, "Father, may I take it?" The old man, looking at him with astonishment, said, "Did you put it there?" "No," the brother replied. "How then," continued the old man, "can you take up something that you did not put down?"

12. Someone asked the old man, "I have received a command, but there is danger of temptation in the place connected with it.

Because of the command I wish to do it, but I am afraid of such danger." The old man said to him, "If this were my problem, I would fulfill the commandment and thus I would overcome the temptation."

13. People said that Father Agathon lived for three years with a stone in his mouth, until he had learned to keep silence.

14. It was said of Agathon and of Father Amoun that, when they had anything to sell, they would name the price just once and silently accept in peace what was given them. Just as, when they wished to buy something, they gave in silence the price they were asked and took the object without any more talk.

15. Whenever his thoughts urged him to pass judgment on something he saw, he would say to himself, "Agathon, it is not your business to do that." In this way, he always recalled his spirit to himself.

16. Agathon said, "Even if a person raises the dead but is full of anger, that person is not acceptable to God."

17. Someone asked Father Agathon about sexual sins. Agathon answered, "Go, tell God about your weakness, and you will find peace."

18. Father Agathon said, "If someone were especially dear to me, but I realized that he was leading me to do something wrong, I would keep that person out of my sight."

19. He also said, "A person ought at all times to be aware of God's judgments."

20. One day some people were talking about charity. Father Joseph said, "Do we really know what charity is?" Then he told a story about a brother who came to see Father Agathon. The Father greeted him and would not let him go until the brother had taken with him one of Agathon's small knives.

21. Agathon said, "If I could meet a leper, give him my body, and take his, I should be very happy." That indeed is perfect charity.

22. People also said of Father Agathon that, coming to the town one day to sell his wares, he encountered a sick traveler lying in the public place without anyone to look after him. The old man rented a room and lived with him there, working with his hands to pay the rent, and spending the rest of his money on the sick man's needs. He stayed there four months until the sick man was restored to health. Then he returned in peace to his prayer chamber.

23. People said that Father Agathon forced himself to fulfill all the commandments. When he sailed in a boat, he was the first to handle the oars. When the brothers came to see him, he set the table with his own hands, as soon as they had prayed, because he was full of God's love. When he was at the point of death, he remained three days with his eyes fixed, wide-open. The brothers roused him, saying, "Father Agathon, where are you?" He replied, "I am standing before the judgment seat of God." They said, "Aren't you afraid, Father?" He replied, "Until this moment, I have done my best to keep God's commandments; but I am a man; how should I know if my deeds are acceptable to God?" The brothers said to him, "Don't you have confidence that you have lived your life according to the God's law?" The old man replied, "I won't have any confidence until I meet God. Truly God's judgment is not human judgment." When they wanted to question him further, he said to them, "Don't talk to me anymore about your charity, for I no longer have time." So he died with joy. They saw him depart like one greeting his dearest friends. He preserved the strictest watchfulness in all things, saying, "Without great watchfulness a person does not advance in even a single virtue."

24. Going to town one day to sell some small articles, on the roadside Agathon met a cripple, who asked him where he was

going. Agathon replied, "To town, to sell some things." The other said, "Please carry me there with you." So he carried him to the town. The cripple said to him, "Put me down where you sell your wares." Agathon did so. When he had sold an article, the cripple asked, "What did you sell it for?" And he told him the price. The other said, "Buy me a cake," and he bought it. When Agathon had sold a second article, the sick man asked, "How much did you sell it for?" And he told him the price of it. Then the other said, "Buy me this," and he bought it. When Agathon, having sold all his wares, wanted to go, the sick man said to him, "Are you going back?" and he replied, "Yes." Then the paralyzed man said, "Please carry me back to the place where you found me." Once more picking him up, Agathon carried him back to that place. Then the cripple said, "Agathon, you are filled with divine blessings, in heaven and on earth." Raising his eyes, Agathon saw no man; it was an angel of the Lord, come to try him.

✠

MOSES

1. One day Father Moses was struggling with the temptation of sexual sin. Unable to stay any longer in his prayer chamber, he went and told Father Isidore. The old man urged him to return to his room. But Moses refused, saying, "Father, I cannot." Then Isidore took Moses out onto the terrace and said to him, "Look toward the west." He looked and saw hordes of demons flying about and making a noise before launching an attack. Then Isidore said to him, "Look toward the east." He turned and saw an innumerable multitude of holy angels shining with glory. Father Isidore said, "See, the Lord sends the

angels to the saints to bring them help, while those in the west fight against them. Those who are with us are more numerous than they are." Then Moses gave thanks to God, plucked up courage, and returned to his prayer chamber.

2. One of the brothers committed a sin. Moses was invited to attend a council about this, but he refused to go. Then a priest sent someone to say to him, "Come, for everyone is waiting for you." So he got up and went. He took a leaking jug, filled it with water and carried it with him. The others came out to meet him and said to him, "What is this, Father?" The old man said to them, "My sins run out behind me, and I do not see them, and today I am coming to judge the errors of another." When they heard that they said no more to the brother, but forgave him.

3. One of the brothers came to visit Father Moses and asked him to give him a valuable teaching. The old man said, "Go, sit in your room in solitude, and your room will teach you everything."

4. Father Moses said, "The person who leaves the hurried life of the world and lives in solitude is like a bunch of grapes that the sun ripens. The person who remains in the world is like an unripe grape."

5. Father Moses said, "We must die to our neighbors and never judge them at all, in any way whatever."

6. Father Moses said, "If a person does not admit in his heart that he is a sinner, God will not hear him." Someone asked him, "What does that mean, to admit in his heart that he is a sinner?" Then the old man said, "When someone is occupied with his own faults, he does not see those of his neighbor."

7. Father Moses said, "If a person's deeds do not match his prayers, he labors in vain." Someone asked, "What is this harmony between practice and prayer?" The old man said, "We

should no longer do those things against which we pray. For when a person gives up his own will, then God is reconciled with him and accepts his prayers. It is written, *God is our refuge and strength, a very present help in trouble*" (Psalm 46:1).

8. Someone asked Moses, "What good is fasting?" The old man said, "It makes the soul humble. For it is written, *Consider my affliction and my trouble, and forgive all my sins* (Psalm 25:18). So if the soul gives itself all this hardship, God will have mercy on it."

9. Someone asked the old man, "What should a person do about all the temptations and evil thoughts that come to him?" He replied, "The person should weep and beg for God's goodness to help him. He will find peace if he prays with discernment. For it is written, *With the Lord on my side I do not fear. What can mortals do to me?*" (Psalm 118:6).

10. Father Moses said, "Bear your own faults and do not pay attention to anyone else, wondering whether they are good or bad. Do not harm anyone; do not harbor evil thoughts in your heart toward anyone; do not condemn the person who commits evil; do not have confidence in the person who does wrong to his neighbor; do not rejoice with the one who injures his neighbor. Do not agree with the one who slanders his neighbor, and do not hate the one who slanders his neighbor. This is what it means not to judge. Do not harbor hostile feelings toward anyone, and do not let malice dominate your heart. This is what peace is. Encourage yourself with this thought: Affliction lasts only a short time, while peace is forever, by the grace of God's Word.

✠

POEMEN (CALLED THE SHEPHERD)

1. Someone questioned Father Poemen, saying, "I have committed a great sin, and I want to do penance for three years." The old man said to him, "That is a lot." The person said, "For one year?" The old man said again, "That is a lot." Those who were present said, "For forty days?" He said again, "That is a lot." He added, "I myself say that if a man repents with his whole heart and does not intend to commit the sin any more, God will accept him after only three days."

2. Poemen said, "If someone shuts a snake and a scorpion up in a bottle, in time they will be completely destroyed. So it is with evil thoughts: They are suggested by the demons; they disappear through patience."

3. He also said, "Experience is a good thing; it tests a man."

4. He also said, "A person who teaches without doing what he teaches is like a spring that cleanses and gives drink to everyone, but is not able to purify itself."

5. He also said, "A man may seem to be silent, but if he condemns others in his heart he is babbling ceaselessly. But there may be another person who talks from morning until night, and yet he is truly silent; that is, he says nothing that is not profitable."

6. Someone else questioned him: "What does this mean: *See that none of you repays evil for evil?*" (1 Thessalonians 5:15). The old man said to him, "Passions work in four stages: first, in the heart; second, in the face; third, in words; and fourth, it is essential not to render evil for evil in deeds. If you can purify your heart, passion will not come into your expression. But if it comes into your face, take care not to speak; but if you do speak, cut the conversation short, in case you render evil for evil."

7. Father Poemen said, "Watchfulness, self-knowledge, and discernment: These are the guides of the soul."

8. He also said, "All bodily comfort is an abomination to the Lord."

9. He also said, "The beginning of evil is ignorance."

10. Father Poemen said, "Even if a person were to make a new heaven and earth, he could not live free of care."

11. He also said, "Just as a person's breath comes out of his nostrils, so does a person need humility and the fear of God."

12. Father Poemen said that Father Ammonas said, "A person can spend his whole time carrying an axe without succeeding in cutting down the tree. Another person, who has experience in chopping down trees, brings the tree down with a few blows. He said that the axe is discernment."

13. He also said, "Poverty, hardship, rigor, and fasting are the instruments of the solitary life. It is written: *When these three men are together, Noah, Job, and Daniel, there am I, says the* LORD (cf. Ezekiel 14.14). Noah represents poverty; Job, suffering; and Daniel, discernment. So, if these three works are found in a person, the Lord dwells in that person."

14. Father Poemen said, "Teach your mouth to say that which you have in your heart."

15. He also said, "Do not give your heart to that which does not satisfy your heart."

16. He also said, "If you take little account of yourself, you will have peace, wherever you live."

17. He also said, "When self-will and ease become habitual, they overthrow a person."

18. He also said, "If you are silent, you will have peace wherever you live."

19. Father Poemen said that blessed Father Antony used to say, "The greatest thing a man can do is to throw his faults before the Lord and to expect temptation to his last breath."

20. Someone asked Father Poemen, "Is it better to speak or to be silent?" The old man said to him, "The man who speaks for God's sake does well; but he who is silent for God's sake also does well."

21. Poemen said, "These three things are the most helpful of all: fear of the Lord, prayer, and doing good to one's neighbor."

22. He also said, "A person who stays in his place in life will not be troubled."

23. He also said, "Teach your heart to guard what your tongue teaches."

24. He also said, "If a man understands something and does not practice it, how can he teach it to his neighbor?"

25. He also said, "Not understanding what has happened prevents us from going on to something better."

26. He also said, "Do not lay open your conscience to anyone whom you do not trust in your heart."